...And There Was Light

ב״ה

...And There Was Light

A Photographic Chronicle
of the Public Chanukah Menorah Celebrations
Sponsored by Chabad-Lubavitch
Around the World

Published by
Merkos L'inyonei Chinuch
770 Eastern Parkway
Brooklyn, New York 11213

5748 • 1987
שנת הקהל

Merkos L'Inyonei Chinuch
770 Eastern Parkway
Brooklyn, New York 11213
(718) 774-4000

Library of Congress Cataloging-in-Publication Data

...And there was light:
A photographic chronicle of the public Chanukah menorah celebrations
sponsored by Chabad-Lubavitch around the world.

1. Chabad Lubavitch (Organization)–Pictorial works.
2. Hanukkah–Pictorial works. I. Chabad Lubavitch (Organization)

BM198.A53 1987   296.8'33   87-5604

ISBN 0-8266-0379-3

Graphic Design
Asher Hecht
Avrohom Weg

Printed in the United States of America

Table of Contents

"...Chanukah, the Festival of Lights, recalls the victory—more than 2100 years ago—of a militarily weak but spiritually strong Jewish people over the mighty forces of a ruthless enemy that had overrun the Holy Land and threatened to engulf the land and its people in darkness.

The miraculous victory—culminating with the rededication of the Sanctuary in Jerusalem and the rekindling of the Menorah which had been desecrated and extinguished by the enemy—has been celebrated annually ever since during these eight days of Chanukah, especially by lighting the Chanukah Menorah, also as a symbol and message of the triumph of freedom over oppression, of spirit over matter, of light over darkness.

It is a timely and reassuring message, for the forces of darkness are ever present. Moreover, the danger does not come exclusively from outside; it often lurks close to home, in the form of insidious erosion of time-honored values and principles that are the foundation of any decent human society. Needless to say, darkness is not chased away by brooms and sticks, but by illumination. Our Sages said, "A little light expels a lot of darkness."

The Chanukah Lights remind us in a most obvious way that illumination begins at home, within oneself and one's family, by increasing and intensifying the light of the Torah and Mitzvos in the everyday experience, even as the Chanukah Lights are kindled in growing numbers from day to day. But though it begins at home, it does not stop there. Such is the nature of light that when one kindles a light for one's own benefit, it benefits also all who are in the vicinity. Indeed, the Chanukah Lights are expressly meant to illuminate the "outside," symbolically alluding to the duty to bring light also to those who, for one reason or another, still walk in darkness.

What is true of the individual is true of a nation, especially this great United States, united under G-d, and generously blessed by G-d with material as well as spiritual riches. It is surely the duty and privilege of this Nation to promote all the forces of light both at home and abroad, and in a steadily growing measure..."

From a letter by
the Lubavitcher Rebbe
Rabbi Menachem M. Schneerson שליט״א

...And There
Was Light

Chanukah, the "Festival of Lights," is a celebration of a great miracle—the victory of a small, beleaguered Jewish nation over its powerful oppressors. In lighting the menorah, we rejoice in the triumph of freedom over tyranny, good over evil, right over might, light over darkness. The menorah proclaims to all that through our dedication and devotion, the light of goodness and holiness can never be obscured, that darkness will ultimately be banished forever.

Chanukah 5747 (1986-7) may have been the most widely celebrated, the most publicly proclaimed Chanukah in history. Throughout the world, in great cities and small villages, in town squares and shopping malls, alongside highways and byways and waterways, the "lamplighters" of the Chabad-Lubavitch movement kindled menorahs—in many cases, towering, giant menorahs—in public places for all to see.

This book is a photographic chronicle of these events. Compiled at the behest of the Lubavitcher Rebbe, Rabbi Menachem M. Schneerson שליט״א, it is intended not merely as testimony to the

Some of the Chabad-Lubavitch emissaries at the Shluchim Conference held annually at Lubavitch World Headquarters (background).

indefatigable efforts of the Rebbe's emissaries, but as a source of inspiration, a catalyst for continued efforts and increasing success in the task of spreading spiritual light.

A Lesson in Religious Freedom

It was more than 2100 years ago that the small Jewish nation overthrew the mighty Syrian-Greeks to regain control of the Holy Land. In celebration, every Jew was enjoined to place a menorah outside his home to "publicize the miracle" of the victory over religious persecution. But as the light of their freedoms dimmed and Jews were once again forced to live in lands of bigotry and persecution, the public menorah lights, cowering from the winds of religious hatred, were forced into their homes.

A Land of Liberty

Now, in a land that vigorously protects the right of every man to practice his religion freely, Jews are once again lighting menorahs in public to proclaim the universal message of religious freedom. These public lightings confirm the basic beliefs of America's first settlers, themselves victims of

The "National Menorah," which stands in front of the White House, in Washington, D.C.

THE WHITE HOUSE

WASHINGTON

January 22, 1987

Dear Rabbi Shemtov:

I was delighted to accept the handsome
menorah from you and your fellow rabbis
when you came to the White House for the
third consecutive year. Thank you very
much for this spiritual gift -- and for
the copy of <u>Let There Be Light</u> which you
also presented to me. I am particularly
pleased to have these special remembrances
in observance of Hanukkah -- and your
organization's steadfast support and
friendship mean more than I can say.

Please convey my kindest regards to the
Lubavitcher Rebbe, Rabbi Schneerson. You
and all the American Friends of Lubavitch
have my best wishes.

Sincerely,

Ronald Reagan

Rabbi Abraham Shemtov
National Director
American Friends of Lubavitch
7622 Castor Avenue
Philadelphia, Pennsylvania 19152

religious persecution. Indeed, freedom to practice religion became inscribed in the laws of the land: "Congress shall make no law respecting the establishment of religion, or prohibiting the free exercise thereof."

This First Amendment to the Constitution guarantees individuals the right to practice their religion without fear, and prevents the government from favoring any particular faith. Indeed, the Supreme Court has recently stated that *The Constitution affirmatively mandates accommodation, not merely tolerance, of all religions."*

The public menorahs symbolize this spirit of liberty and have thus won a place not only in Jewish life but also in the life of the American people.

Chanukah: A Lesson In Education

Chanukah also focuses public concern on the importance of education in creating and sustaining a strong, vibrant, creative and moral society. In fact, the very word "Chanukah" means education. The lessons of Chanukah confirm the American belief that education is the essential component of a free and moral society, the guarantor of a better future for everyone.

On December 22, 1986, ten emissaries of the Rebbe met with President Reagan in the Oval Office, the eighth annual exchange of greetings between the Rebbe and the President of the United States. They presented him with a silver menorah and a copy of *Let There Be Light,* the pictorial chronicle of the Lubavitch Chanukah activities for 1985. The President reiterated his support of the Rebbe's efforts to improve the quality of education worldwide, and echoed his call for adherance to the Universal Moral Code–the Seven Noahide Laws.

Lights To The World

These menorahs, first displayed publicly in America, now light up thousands of cities and communities around the world. They now burn brightly, proclaiming the universal message of religious freedom, in countries where they would be unacceptable only a few years ago.

May these menorahs continue to illuminate the pathways to freedom for all mankind.

I
North America

UNITED STATES OF AMERICA
CANADA

Alabama

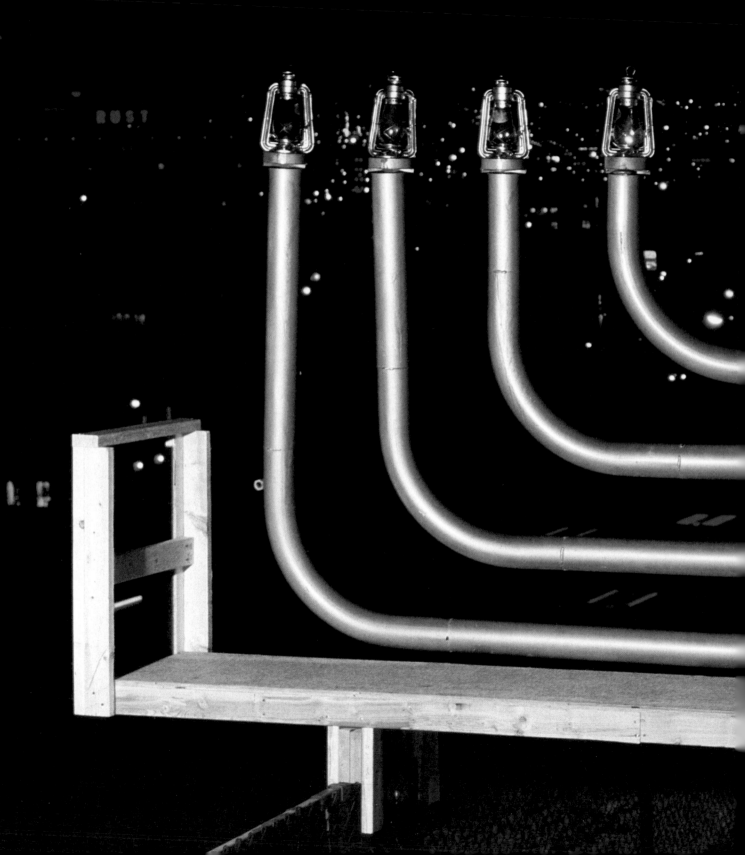

Previous page:
BIRMINGHAM. Rabbi Y. M. Lipszycz, Director of Chabad-Lubavitch activities in Alabama, readies this giant menorah for kindling. The menorah overlooks Red Mountain Expressway, a major thoroughfare linking downtown Birmingham with outlying suburban areas.

Facing page:
BIRMINGHAM. After being lit, the menorah telescopes high above the Expressway, publicizing the miracle of Chanukah in a spectacular manner.

Top:
MONTGOMERY. Rabbi Lipszycz hosts a Chanukah party and discussion in the Montgomery Chabad House.

Bottom:
Lighting the menorah outside the Chabad House.

Arizona

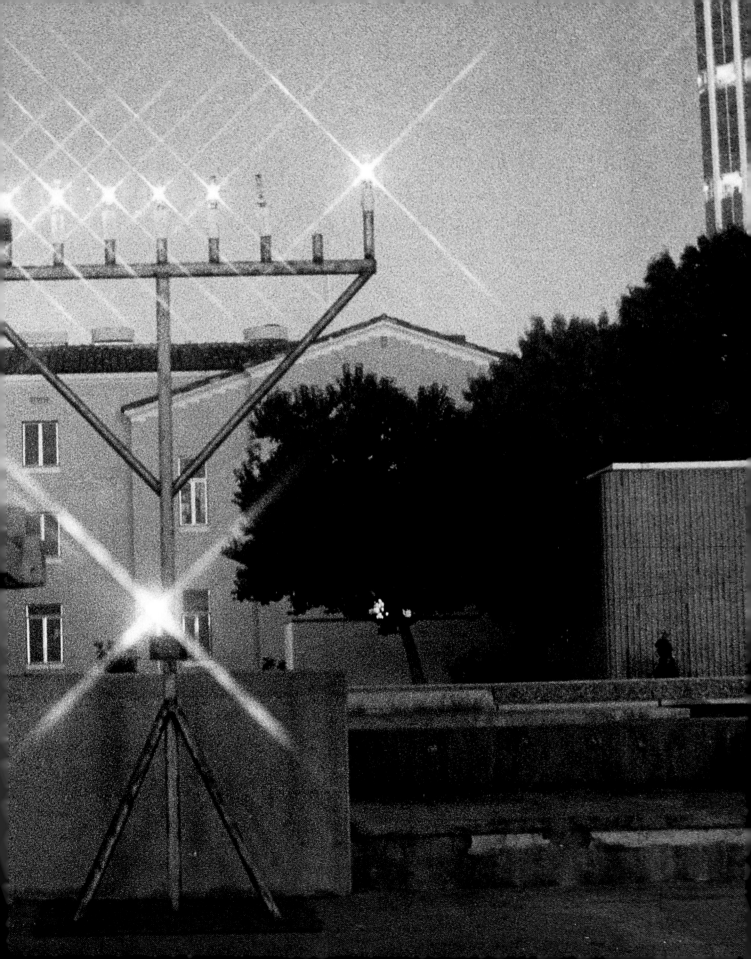

Previous page:
TUSCON. The public menorah in El Presidio Park.

PHOENIX. A Sunday Chanukah gathering at Phoenix Civic Plaza.

Top:
TEMPE. A Tempe children's choir sings Chanukah songs.

Bottom:
On the second night of Chanukah, youngsters spread the light at the Phoenix Jewish Community Center.

California

Previous page
Designed by world-renowned artist Yaacov
Agam, this remarkable menorah stands
proud in the heart of Beverly Hills.

Below:
S. ANA. Rabbi David Eliezrie, Director of
Chabad-Lubavitch activities in Anaheim,
with his daughter Naomi, lights the public
menorah in Sasscer Park, at the Orange
County Civic Center.

Facing page:
AGOURA. Rabbi Moshe Bryski and
Hollywood star Philip Glasser light the giant
menorah in Agoura Hills City Mall. **Insets:**
(Left) Representatives of various countries
grasp the "Torch of Unity", symbolizing the
oneness of world Jewry. **(Right)** Agoura
Hills Mayor James W. Koenig presents
Chabad rabbis with a proclamation naming
the week of Chanukah as "Chabad Week".

Right:
BEVERLY HILLS. Internationally renowned artist Yaacov Agam explains the basis of his striking menorah design.

Below:
More than three thousand attended the lighting ceremony at Beverly Gardens Park, across the street from Beverly Hills City Hall.

Facing page:
Agam's "Chabad Freedom Menorah", standing twenty-seven feet tall and weighing nearly three tons, dominates the landscape.

Top:

BRAWLEY. Dozens of menorahs were kindled in various communities throughout California. This one is in front of City Hall in Brawley, near S. Diego.

Bottom:
BEL AIR. Part of the crowd attending an open-air celebration on the night of the sixth light of Chanukah.

Top:
BRENTWOOD. Rabbi Boruch Hecht and congregant with the Chabad menorah at a local shopping center.

Bottom:
CENTURY CITY. A Chabad boys choir entertains the Chanukah celebrants at a Century City mall.

IRVINE. One of three giant menorahs instilling Jewish pride among the residents of this southern California community.

MOJAVE DESERT. Some of the celebrants enjoying a Chanukah party at Edwards Air Force Base.

LA JOLLA. The third light of Chanukah drew this happy group to an outdoor celebration at Devenshire Art Gallery.

THE ORANGE COUNTY
Register

January 13, 1987

Chabad of Laguna member Steve Edwards lights the menorah erected by his temple in Laguna Beach.

Right:
LOS ANGELES. The century-old brass Katowitz menorah, six feet tall and hand-wrought, was spirited out of war-torn Poland during the Holocaust. Since 1983 it has been displayed each Chanukah in the rotunda of Los Angeles City Hall.

Facing page, top:
Rabbi Boruch Shlomo Cunin, Director of West Coast Chabad-Lubavitch, kindles the menorah on the steps of City Hall.

Bottom:
Hollywood screen actor Elliot Gould lights the public menorah at Farmer's Market in Los Angeles, as Rabbi Cunin and local merchants look on.

Right:
MARINA DEL REY. Rabbi Shmuel Naparstek officiates at a menorah lighting in Burton W. Chase Park.

Below:
LOMITA. South Bay children share Chanukah joy with a City Hall Administrator.

Left:
CORTE MADERA. Rabbi Chaim Dalfin, Director of
Chabad-Lubavitch activities in Marin County,
asists youngsters in performing the mitzvah of
kindling menorahs.

Below:
RANCHO BERNARDO. The kosher foods section
of Ralph's Shopping Center features a "special" on
Chanukah spirit.

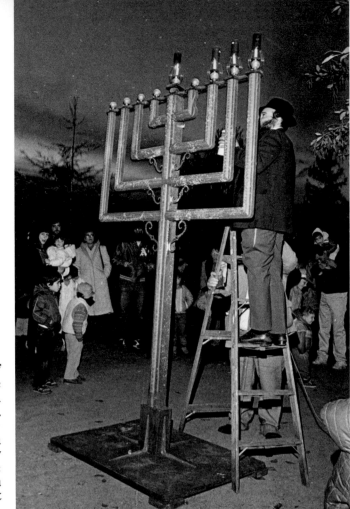

Right:
S. JOSE. Rabbi Yosef Levin, Director of
Chabad-Lubavitch activities on the
Peninsula, kindling the menorah at Parma
Park.
Below:
PALO ALTO. The children of Chabad's Gan
Yeladim Nursery present a Chanukah play
Facing page:
At the menorah lighting ceremony in Lytton
Plaza in downtown Palo Alto, every child felt
lucky to receive a *dreidle* from Rabbi Levin.

S. BARBARA. The crowd begins to gather for a public Chanukah celebration at a S. Barbara mall.

S. MONICA. At a Chanukah party, this young man discovers that there is more than one way to spread the light.

Rabbi Shlomo Menkes lights the public menorah at S. Monica's Palisades Park.

Facing page:
PALM DESERT. Mayor Jeffrey Bleaman of Rancho Mirage lights the menorah at the Town Center. At his side is Rabbi Yonason Denebeim, Director of Chabad-Lubavitch activities in the Palm Springs area.

Previous pages:
Left:
SHERMAN OAKS. The S. Fernando Valley's most popular shopping center was the site of Chabad of the Valley's grand celebration, "Chanukah at the Galleria". Festivities included singing, dancing, distribution of Chanukah delicacies and toys, and the dramatic kindling of a twenty-five foot tall menorah.

Right:
Television and motion picture actor Steven Furst, and child star Philip Glasser, are hoisted to the top of the menorah for the lighting ceremony. Afterwards, the thousands in attendance recited the "Shema Yisrael" together, word by word.

Facing page:
Top left:
THOUSAND OAKS. Visitors to this Chabad display at Thousand Oaks Mall during the eight days of the festival received menorahs, informative literature, and a healthy measure of Chanukah joy.

Top right:
S. DIEGO. Rabbi Yisroel Goldstein, Director of Chabad-Lubavitch activities in Rancho Bernardo, at the public menorah in front of S. Diego Courthouse.

Bottom left:
S. PEDRO. The Public Library was the site of this Chanukah celebration for local children.

Bottom right:
TORRANCE. A Chanukah lesson in Town Mall.

Below:
VENTURA. Chanukah 1986 marked the first public menorah lighting in the Buenaventura Plaza—the area's largest shopping mall.

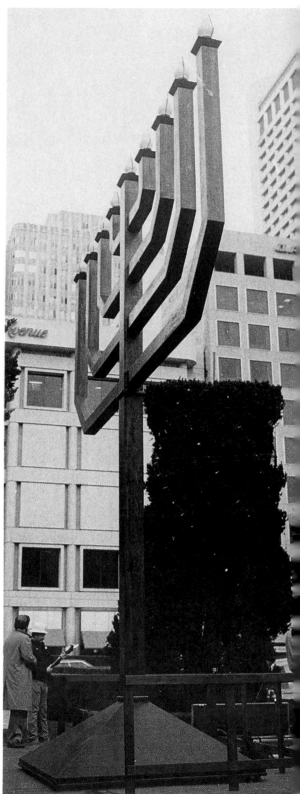

Previous pages:
Left:
S. FRANCISCO. Rabbi Yosef Langer, Director of Chabad-Lubavitch activities in Northern California, passes the torch used to light the menorah in the Twelfth Annual Union Square Chanukah Celebration. In 1975, this was the site of the first public Chanukah observance ever held outside the land of Israel.

Right:
Union Square's twenty-two-foot mahogany menorah was the gift of impresario Bill Graham. Among Californians, it is affectionately known as the "Mama Menorah", because it has spawned so many other public menorahs throughout the world.

Left:
CENTURY CITY. Chabad's "Mobile Menorahs" traveled far and wide, publicizing the miracles of Chanukah everywhere they went.

Colorado

COLORADO SPRINGS
GAZETTE TELEGRAPH

A FREEDOM
NEWSPAPER

115TH YEAR

Lights of Hanukkah

Jarlene Bennett/Gazette Telegraph

Rabbi Mendy Teitlebaum lights the fifth candle, representing the fifth day of Hanukkah, on an 8½-foot menorah outside the First Federal Building at North Academy and Carefree Circle Tuesday. The menorah will be displayed through Friday.

Facing page:
Top:
DENVER. City Auditor Mike Licht, with Rabbi Yisroel Engel, lights the giant menorah at downtown Denver's 16th Street Mall.

Bottom:
Some of the children from the local chapter of Tzivos Hashem who performed at Denver's public Chanukah celebrations.

Connecticut

Right:
BLOOMFIELD. With the public menorah at Town Hall are Bloomfield Mayor David Baram (center), Mr. Larry Cohen of Connecticut Friends of Chabad (left), and Rabbi Chaim Gurevitch of the Chabad House of Greater Hartford.

Following page:
HARTFORD. Rabbi Gurevitch kindles a seventeen-foot menorah in front of the Old State House.

Top:
NEW HAVEN. New England's largest public menorah stands twenty feet tall on the New Haven Green.

Bottom:
Rabbi Pesach Sperlin of the Lubavitch Youth Organization and New Haven Mayor Biagio DiLieto prepare to ignite the Chanukah lights.

Previous page:
HAMDEN. At the Hamden Mart Shopping Center, Rabbi Moshe Hecht, Headmaster of the New Haven Hebrew Day School-Lubavitch, and Rabbi Yaacov Kaploun, flank Mr. Harry Kramer of Kramer Iron Works, who designed and built the menorah. Lighting the menorah is Rabbi Sheya Hecht.

Top:
ORANGE. Rabbi Moshe Hecht with some of the students at New Haven Hebrew Day School-Lubavitch.

Bottom:
TRUMBULL. (Left to right) Rabbi I. Stock, Director of Yeshiva Achei Tmimim-Lubavitch, Rabbi Y.Y. Stock, and Rabbi Y. Torenheim.

Delaware

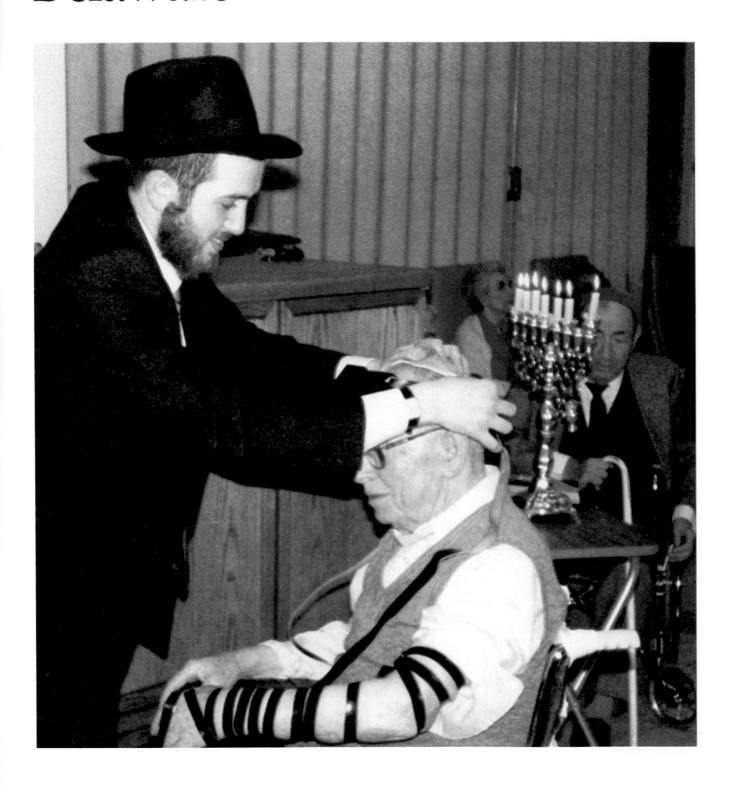

Facing page:
NEWARK. The newly arrived Director of
Chabad-Lubavitch activities in Delaware,
Rabbi Elchanon Vogel, helps an elderly
gentleman at a local old age home
perform two *mitzvot.* A Chanukah
gathering at the new Chabad House
(left); and a cheerful song at the old age
home (bottom).

Florida

MIAMI BEACH. The Giant Chabad-Lubavitch menorah at the Miami Beach City Hall.

Mr. Joe Tanenbaum accepts a medal presented by the mayor of Miami Beach, at a Chanukah rally. Standing from left: Rabbi Abraham Korf, Regional Director of Chabad-Lubavitch activities in Florida; Miami Beach Mayor Alex Daoud; City Commisioner Sid Weisburd; Mr. Tanenbaum and City Commisioner Abe Resnick.

HOLLYWOOD. Despite a relentless downpour, more than 1000 people gathered at the annual Grand Chanukah Festival held at the Young Circle band shell.

HOLLYWOOD. Mayor Mara Guilanti, with Rabbi Raphael Tenenhaus, Director of Chabad-Lubavitch activities in Hollywood, at a Chanukah ceremony in City Hall.

HALLANDALE. At a menorah-lighting ceremony in City Hall, from left: Commisioner Nat Cutler, Rabbi Tenenhaus, Hallandale Vice Mayor Sonny Rosenberg, and Commissioner Colonel Phil Cohen.

HALLANDALE. On the parking lot of Congregation Levi Yitzchak—Lubavitch, facing busy Hallandale Boulevard, the menorah is lit 20 minutes before sunset on Friday afternoon (right). WEST PALM BEACH. At Cross County Mall, Rabbi Yossi Biston, Director of Chabad-Lubavitch activities in Palm Beach County, speaks to a group of children on the significance of Chanukah (bottom).

SARASOTA. Mayor K. Kirshner and Rabbi Alter Bukiet, Director of the Chabad-Lubavitch Center in Sarasota, address the crowd at the city's first public menorah lighting ceremony, which took place at Bayfront Park (left); and a section of the crowd (bottom).

TAMPA. At the menorah lighting ceremony at City Hall Plaza, Mayor Sandy Friedman and Rabbi Yossie Dubrowski, Director of Chabad-Lubavitch activities in Tampa (right). ORLANDO. Rabbi Sholom B. Dubov, Director of Chabad-Lubavitch activities in Orlando, leads a "L'Chayim" at a Chabad House get-together (bottom).

Georgia

ATLANTA. As Jan Seigelman lights the Chabad-Lubavitch menorah at Perimeter Mall, the crowd gathers to learn more about Chanukah.

Illinois

CHICAGO. The giant 18-foot Chabad-
Lubavitch menorah at Daley Plaza.

CHICAGO. Rabbi Daniel Moscowitz, Director of Chabad-Lubavitch activities in Illinois, Alderman Jerome Orbach, and Menorah Project Chairman Alfred Von Samek kindle the menorah on Daley Plaza (above); while, on the ground "Judah Maccabee" joins the dancing (right).
Facing page:
HIGHLAND PARK. Among the more innovative projects of North Suburban Lubavitch-Chabad was this "Dreidel House," complete with a costumed "Judah Maccabee" — alias Rabbi Yosef Schanowitz, director of Chabad-Lubavitch activities in Highland Park. The House, which stood at Crossroads Shopping Center, attracted thousands of visitors, young and old, each of whom left with a better understanding of the festival of Chanukah, its history, and significance.

HIGHLAND PARK. The North Suburban
Lubavitch-Chabad menorah (right).
CHICAGO. One of the city's many car-top
menorahs (bottom).

EVANSTON. Rabbi Dov Hillel Klein, Director of the Tanenbaum Chabad House in Evanston, lights the menorah outside the Chabad House (left). CHICAGO. Rabbi Shmuel Notik, Director of the Chicago branch of Friends of Refugees of Eastern Europe, with a group of young recently-arrived Russian children, who are seeing a menorah for what may be the very first time in their lives (bottom).

Indiana

INDIANAPOLIS. Rabbi A. Grossbaum, Director of Chabad-Lubavitch activities in Indiana, kindles the menorah in front of the State Capitol (facing page), in downtown Indianapolis (far left), and at the Indiana World War Memorial (left). At the Park Regency Senior Citizen's Residence (bottom), Rabbi Grossbaum poses with some of the participants in a Chanukah program.

Iowa

DES MOINES. On the steps of the Iowa State Capitol, this public menorah stands as a proud symbol of liberty.

Kentucky

LOUISVILLE. Rabbi Avrohom Litvin, Director of Chabad-Lubavitch activities in Kentucky, is assisted by Martin Goldsmith in lighting the car-top menorah. At bottom, Rabbi Litvin addresses the assembled children and parents on the significance of Chanukah.

Louisiana

NEW ORLEANS. Rabbi Zelig Rivkin, Director of Chabad-Lubavitch activities in Louisiana, lights the menorah at the Chabad House Chanukah Rally under the watchful eyes of some young citizens.

An art contest at the Chanukah rally (above); and at right, members of Tzivos Hashem visit with the Willowood Jewish Home for the Aged.

The Chabad Mobile Menorah joins the Sugar Bowl visitors in New Orleans' famous French Quarter. At the Chanukah rally, the children bake their own Chanukah cookies (below).

Maryland

COLUMBIA. On the third night of Chanukah, local residents gathered in downtown Columbia to participate in the menorah lighting ceremony (top). ROCKVILLE. Residents of the Revitz House Senior Citizens Center join Chabad House Rabbi Benzion Geisinsky at a Chanukah party (center). BETHESDA. As a choir of youngsters entertains with a special Chanukah repertoire at the Bethesda Metro Center, Rabbi Shmuel Kaplan, Director of Chabad-Lubavitch activities in Maryland, surveys the crowd (bottom).

Facing page:
BALTIMORE. The Chabad menorah aglow in front of City Hall.

Massachusetts

BOSTON. The Chabad-Lubavitch
menorah on Boston Common.
Following Pages:
FRAMINGHAM. Rabbi Yaakov Lazaros
stops traffic as he lights the 10-foot
menorah in front of Town Hall (left).
BOSTON. Mayor Raymond L. Flynn is
assisted in lighting the *Shamash* by
Rabbi Chaim Prus, Director of
Chabad-Lubavitch activities in Greater
Boston, as a crowd gathers to witness the
event.

AMHERST. The Chabad Mobile Menorah, in front of the Town Hall. PITTSFIELD. Mayor Charles Smith and Rabbi Yisroel Deren, Director of Chabad-Lubavitch activities in Western and Southern New England, during a television interview (right), after the menorah lighting ceremony at City Hall (facing page).

Left:
SPRINGFIELD. Rabbi Yisroel Deren, Director of Chabad House in Springfield, lighting the menorah in Court Square, in downtown Springfield.

Below:
Judge David Sacks joins Rabbi Deren in the 'cherrypicker' as they address the crowd.

Inset:
A group of children sing old-time Chanukah favorites at the menorah lighting celebration.

WORCESTER. Rabbi Herschel Fogelman, director of Chabad-Lubavitch activities in Central Massachusetts, and son Levi Fogelman, help workers from Modern Manufacturing and Saxton Sign Company raise the giant menorah at Newton Square.

Facing page:
WORCESTER. Participants at the lighting of the menorah at Newton Square, on the third night of Chanukah, break into a whirling dance around the menorah.
Left:
MAINE. At a ceremony in City Hall, Portland Mayor Ronald J. Dorler accepts a menorah from Rabbi Reuven Pollack, Principal of the Levey Hebrew Day School.
Bottom:
NEW HAMPSHIRE. In Manchester City Hall, Mayor Robert Shaw accepts a menorah from Rabbis Levi Fogelman and Meyer S. Abramowitz of Chabad-Lubavitch of Central Mass.

Michigan

NORTHERN MICHIGAN. This Mobile
Menorah reached across northern
Michigan, bringing the spirit of the
festival to isolated communities where
Chanukah may otherwise never have
been celebrated. Pictured here is a
resident of Hancock enjoying a rare
opportunity to put on Tefillin.

METROPOLITAN DETROIT. Part of a travelling Shabbat exhibit, sponsored by the Lubavitch Women's Organization, which demonstrates the beauty of Shabbat observance (bottom).

FARMINGTON HILLS. Yankel Stark places the *Shamash* into position in the menorah at Lubavitch of Farmington Hills.

FARMINGTON HILLS. Rabbi Chaim Bergstein and Rabbi Yossi Polter, at the menorah in front of Congregation Bais Chabad.

ANN ARBOR. Rabbi Aron Goldstein, Director of Chabad House in Ann Arbor, lights the menorah.

FLINT. At a Chanukah party in a local nursing home, some members of the Tiferes Zekaneim Levi Yitzchok play dreidle while waiting for their latkes.

Facing Page:
GRAND RAPIDS. Calder Plaza was the home for this striking menorah.

HAPPY CHANUKAH TO ALL

Minnesota

S. PAUL. During S. Paul Mayor George Latimer's visit to the Lubavitch Learning Center and its recently installed menorah, Rabbi Moshe Feller, Lubavitch representative to the upper Midwest (center), and Rabbi Shlomo Bendet present the Mayor with a copy of *Let There Be Light* - the pictorial chronicle of the world-wide activities of Lubavitch during the 1985-6 Chanukah season.

Rabbi Gershon Grossbaum of
Lubavitch House lights a 31-foot
menorah in St. Louis Park, at
Minnetonka Boulevard, overlooking
one of Minnesota's busiest freeways.

Students from around the world find a deeper and brighter purpose to their lives during the Chanukah Mid-Winter session at the world-famous Bais Chana Institute in St. Paul.

Rabbi Manis Friedman, principal of Bais Chana Women's Institute, addresses a special Chanukah Rally on the steps of the Minnesota State Capitol in St. Paul.

Missouri

ST. LOUIS. Rabbi Yosef
Landa, Director of
Chabad-Lubavitch activities
in St. Louis, lights up the St.
Louis Government Center in
Clayton, at the tallest
menorah in Missouri.

Rabbi Landa explains the meaning of the Chanukah lights to a group of senior citizens.

Everyone was a winner in this Chanukah game, at a festive children's party held at the St. Louis Chabad House.

KANSAS CITY. Young Levi, Yossi, Chani and Ita–all members of Kansas City's "Tzivos Hashem"–entertain the elderly at the home for Senior Citizens.

Mr. Ronald Dimbert gives a big assist to young Zalman Friedman in lighting the menorah at Chabad House, as Chabad House Director Rabbi Benzion Friedman looks on.

Kansas City Mayor Richard Berkeley lights the giant Chabad House menorah. At lower right is Rabbi Sholom B. Wineberg, Director of Chabad Lubavitch activities in Missouri.

Nebraska

OMAHA. Rabbi Mendel Katzman, director of the newly established Chabad Center in Nebraska, explaining the significance of a publicly displayed menorah to Omaha Mayor M. Boyle.

Some of the proud children who won prizes at the Chabad "Chanukah Fiesta", held at the Jewish County Center. **Below:** Guest speaker Rabbi Benzion Friedman, Director of Chabad House in Kansas City, addresses the "Latke Extravaganza" at the Omaha Chabad House.

New Jersey

TRENTON: This menorah, on the steps of the New Jersey State House, was sponsored by the Rabbinical College Of America-Lubavitch. Kindling the lights is Saul Cooperman, Commissioner of Education; also present was Jane Burgio, New Jersey Secretary of State, representing Governor Kean.

ATLANTIC COUNTY. Rabbi Shmuel Rapaport, Director of Chabad-Lubavitch activities in Atlantic City, and his children, share the joys of Chanukah with some patients at the Betty Bachrach Rehabilitation Center (top).

NEWARK. One of a fleet of Mobile Menorahs, sponsored by the Rabbinical College of America-Lubavitch (right).

Facing page:
BERGEN COUNTY. An advertisement placed by Friends of Lubavitch of Bergen County, demonstrates their commitment to sharing the spirit of Chanukah with the multitudes.

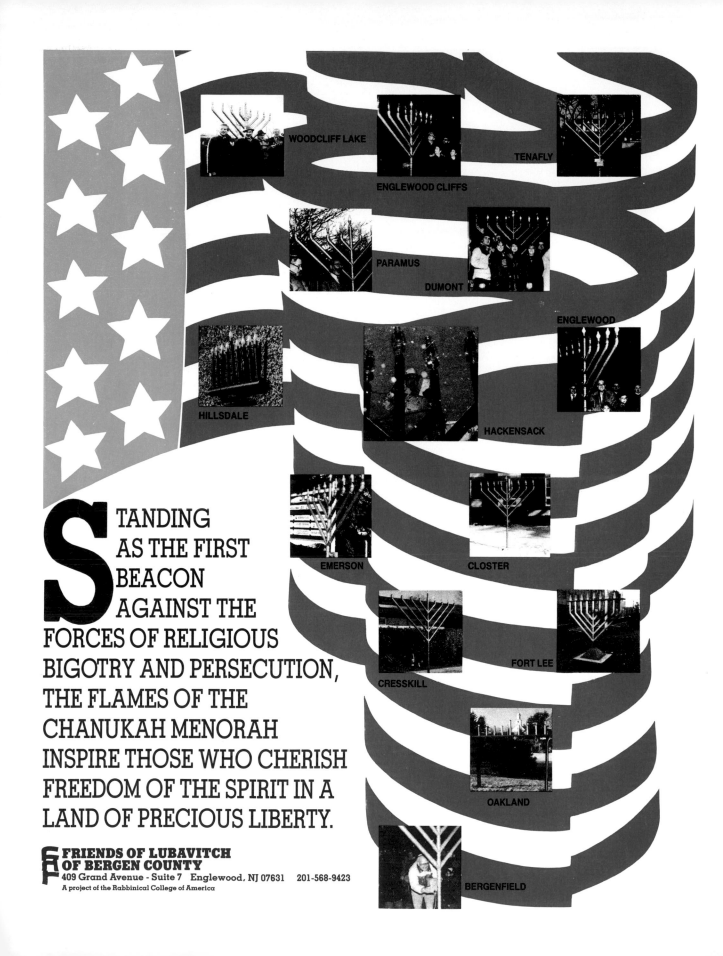

WOODCLIFF LAKE

ENGLEWOOD CLIFFS

TENAFLY

PARAMUS

DUMONT

ENGLEWOOD

HILLSDALE

HACKENSACK

EMERSON

CLOSTER

CRESSKILL

FORT LEE

OAKLAND

BERGENFIELD

STANDING AS THE FIRST BEACON AGAINST THE FORCES OF RELIGIOUS BIGOTRY AND PERSECUTION, THE FLAMES OF THE CHANUKAH MENORAH INSPIRE THOSE WHO CHERISH FREEDOM OF THE SPIRIT IN A LAND OF PRECIOUS LIBERTY.

FRIENDS OF LUBAVITCH OF BERGEN COUNTY
409 Grand Avenue - Suite 7   Englewood, NJ 07631   201-568-9423
A project of the Rabbinical College of America

JERSEY CITY. Sponsored by Bris Avrohom, this menorah at Lincoln Park is lit with the assistance of the local Fire Department and the encouragement of the gathering crowd.

At the menorah lighting ceremony in City Hall, in conjunction with a party honoring Jersey City Mayor Anthony R. Cucci for his commitment to Bris Avrohom are, from left: Rabbi David Wilansky, Administrator of Bris Avrohom; Rabbi Isaac G. Mintz, Educational Director of Bris Avrohom; Chief John Millins of the Fire Department; Mrs. Anthony R. Cucci; Jersey City Mayor Anthony R. Cucci; Rabbi Mordechai Kanelsky, Executive Director of Bris Avrohom; Ralph D'Andrea, chief aid to the Fire Department; Rabbi Boruch Lepkivker, Program Director of Bris Avrohom.

Facing page:
Attorney Herman Silverstein lights the menorah at the Old Hudson County Courthouse, under the watchful eye of young Elana Zaichik.

DEAL. Rabbi Yosef Carlebach, Director of Chabad activities in the New Brunswick area, with Stanley Conover, administrator of Boro of Deal, N.J.

MANALAPAN. After the lighting ceremony at the Manalapan Mall, children line up to receive Chanukah dreidles from Rabbi Boruch Chazanow, Director of Chabad House in Manalapan.

At one of the many menorahs
displayed in supermarkets all around
the county.

MANALAPAN. Barry Kaplan places a
lamp high atop the 16-foot menorah
at Manalapan Mall, as hundreds of
people join in the celebration down on
the ground.

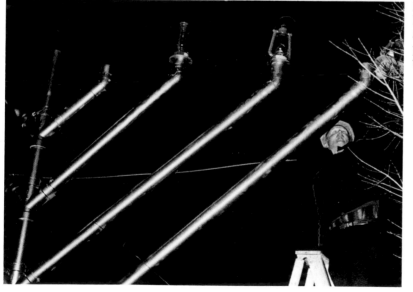

PARSIPPANY. Rabbi Moshe Herson kindles the menorah at the entrance to Powder Mill Village in Parsippany, in the presence of U.S. Congressman Dean Gallo; Village developer Edward Mosberg, his son-in-law Stuart Levine, and other prominent citizens participated.

Rabbi Moshe Herson (right) and Rabbi Israel Gordon, with Parsippany-Troy Hills Mayor Frank Priore, in front of the Parsippany Municipal Building.

NEW BRUNSWICK. Chanukah spirit at City Hall.

New York

NEW YORK. Even the towering skyscrapers at the corner of 5th Ave. and 59th Street could not detract from the commanding presence of this, the world's tallest Chanukah menorah, created by internationally acclaimed artist Yaakov Agam. Thousands came to witness the kindling of the Chanukah lights and enjoy live music, hot latkes and joyous dancing. Lighting the menorah are Rabbi Shmuel Butman, Director Of Lubavitch Youth Organization (left), and Rabbi Dovid Raskin, Chairman of LYO.

NEW YORK CITY. Grand Army Plaza at 5th Ave. and 59th St., the site of the famous 30-foot Agam menorah, attracted thousands of bustling New Yorkers to this Lubavitch Youth Organization "Mitzvah Tank". The visitors were welcomed with piping hot Chanukah *latkes* and *dreidles* for the children.

One of the numerous menorahs placed by the Lubavitch Youth Organization in various locations in the Metropolitan Area. This one is on the Avenue of the Americas.

NEW YORK CITY. At the foot of the Agam menorah, Lubavitch Youth Organization's Rabbi Shlomo Friedman (left) and Rabbi Shmuel Butman shield themselves from icy blasts of snow and sleet, as they are about to be lifted in a cherry-picker to light the menorah.

Artist Yaakov Agam autographs the base of the menorah he created, as Rabbi Shmuel Butman and Rabbi David Raskin, Director and Chairman of Lubavitch Youth Organization, look on.

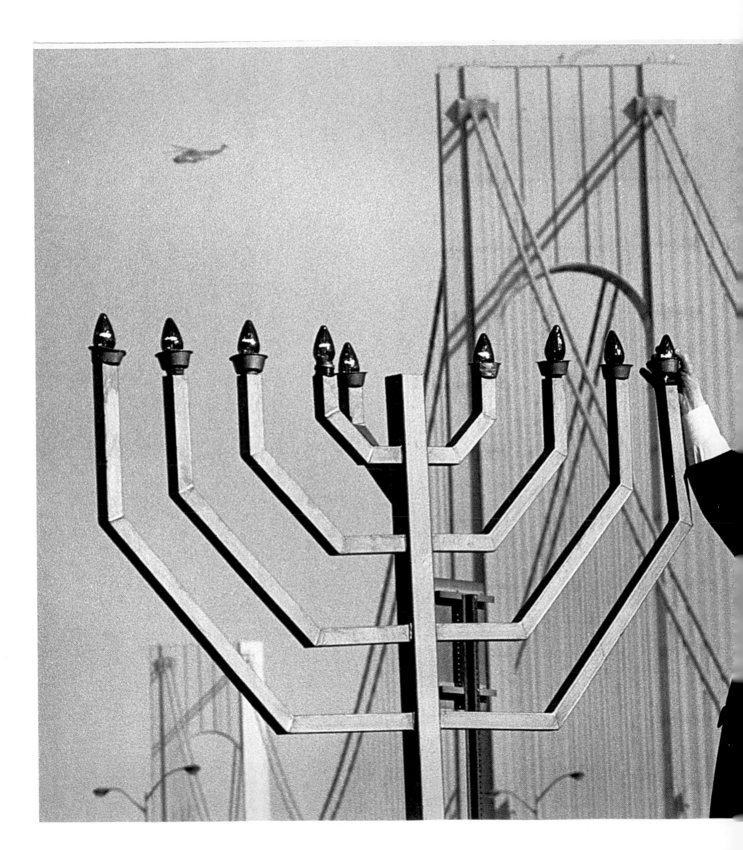

NEW YORK CITY. Rabbi Shmuel Butman lights the Lubavitch Youth Organization menorah at the Verrazano Narrows Bridge. Menorahs were placed at all bridges and tunnels of the N.Y.-N.J. Metropolitan Transit Authority, as well as at the Verrazano, Whitestone and Triborough Bridges and the Brooklyn Battery and Queens Midtown Tunnels.

Standing proudly as the beacon of freedom for all mankind, the Statue of Liberty was accompanied, for the very first time this year, by the menorah—symbolizing the eternal message of Religious Freedom.

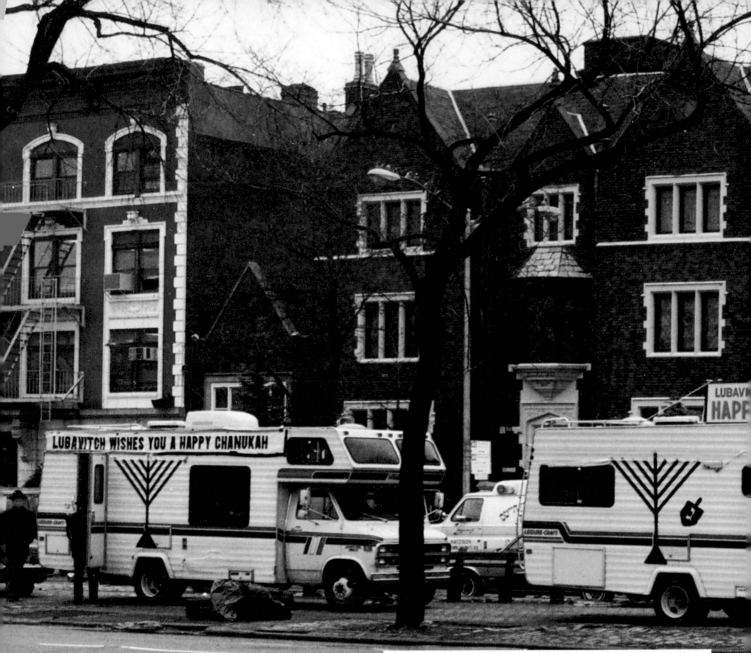

CROWN HEIGHTS, BROOKLYN. In front of the Chabad-Lubavitch World Headquarters, at 770 Eastern Parkway, a cavalcade of 'Mitzvah Tanks' prepares to fan out to all parts of the New York metropolitan area. An estimated 30,000 people received Chanukah kits from the young 'tankists' who manned these mobile units.

Insets:
Not far away from Lubavitch World Headquarters, at Grand Army Plaza, Rabbi Shimon Hecht lights Brooklyn's largest menorah, sponsored by the National Committee for Furtherance of Jewish Education.

ALBANY. Four hundred children attended the grand Lubavitch Chanukah Rally at the State Museum in the State Capitol (right).

BINGHAMTON. Broome County Executive Carl Young addressed a crowd of hundreds of celebrants at the Oakdale Mall, at a menorah-lighting ceremony sponsored by Chabad House of S.U.N.Y. Binghamton.

BROOKLYN. Rabbi Sholom B. Friedman of Milan, Italy, was the guest speaker at a special gathering of recent immigrants from the Soviet Union, held at the Chabad House in Flatbush, Brooklyn. At left is a section of the participants.

BUFFALO. Nobel Prize winner Dr. Herbert Hauptman
braves a Buffalo snow-storm to kindle all eight lights
on the last day of Chanukah.

Right:
Standing in front of the Fire Department cherry-
picker, are, from left: Mayor Griffin of Buffalo; Rabbi
Noson Gurary, Director of Chabad-Lubavitch
activities in Western New York; Erie County Executive
Ed Rutkowski; and Mr. Leonard Rochwerger,
President of the Jewish Welfare Board.

LONG ISLAND. At Suffolk County Headquarters, this
28-foot tall menorah was lit in the presence of County
Executive Michael LaGrande and County Attorney
Marty Ashare.

Even a snow storm didn't stop celebrants from attending candle-lighting at the State University in Stonybrook. Rabbi Michoel Estreicher and Chabad of Suffolk County Director Rabbi Tuvya Teldon (center), bundled up and braved the cold.

EAST END—LONG ISLAND. Rabbi Leibel Baumgarten, Director of Lubavitch activities of East End, together with a group of Tzivos Hashem members, greeting all who came to participate in the Chanukah festivities.

KAUNEONGA. For the first time, a Chanukah menorah shines in the heart of Kauneonga Lake. The menorah was transported over 100 miles for the occasion.

LIBERTY. Mr. Joe Sommer, head manager of Shop-Rite in Liberty, N.Y., welcomed his customers with Chanukah greetings. He was most helpful to Oholei Torah student E. Mintz in placing similar menorahs at various locations in the Catskills.

CORAM. Long Island radio personality Bob Klein was honored with the lighting of the menorah.

NASSAU COUNTY. Busy
Westbury Road was the
home of this handsome
menorah.

ROCKLAND COUNTY. This
menorah weathered the
storm at one of the busiest
intersections in Rockland
County.

NEW CITY. Dr. Mandy Ganchrow was honored with the kindling of this menorah, across from the Nanuet Mall on Route 59 (top).

Mr. Kenneth Zebrowski, Chairman of the Rockland County Legislature, issued a proclamation declaring a "Week Of Religious Freedom". Thanking him is Rabbi Avrohom Kotlarsky, Director of Lubavitch activities in New City (center).

Joel Rosenthal, Mayor of Spring Valley, prepares to kindle the menorah. (bottom).

Facing Page:
Even the snow seemed to dance along, and join in the festive Chanukah spirit.

POUGHKEEPSIE. Outside the Poughkeepsie Municipal Building, Jack Newman lights the 18-foot tall menorah.

Poughkeepsie Mayor Tom Aposporus addressing the crowd, as Rabbi Yacov Borenstein, Director of Chabad of the Mid-Hudson Valley, looks on.

Top:
ROCHESTER. With some assistance from Rabbi Nechemia Vogel, Director of Chabad-Lubavitch activities in Rochester, this little Russian boy lights a menorah for the very first time.

Bottom:
The candle-lighting ceremony in front of the public library, led by Supreme Court Justice Richard D. Rosenbloom.

Top:
SCHENECTADY. Shoppers stopping at the Chanukah exhibit in Schenectady's Mohawk Mall received free menorahs and Chanukah literature.
Left:
Chabad's various Chanukah activities prompted a TV News interview about the holiday, with Rabbi Nathan Gross, Director of Chabad-Lubavitch activities in Schenectady.

SYRACUSE. Mayor Tom Young at the
Chabad-Lubavitch menorah in Hanover
Square.

DE WITT. Rabbi Yaakov T. Rapaport, Director of Lubavitch activities in Syracuse, in a special Chanukah game with a group of children at the Jewish Community Center.

North Carolina

CHARLOTTE. Rabbi Yosef Y. Groner, Director of Lubavitch activities in the Carolinas, extending Happy Chanukah wishes at Shalom Park in Charlotte, North Carolina.

LUBAVITCH WISHES YOU A HAPPY CHANUKAH

South Carolina

Top:
Rabbi and Mrs. Groner and students from the Lubavitch nursery school in Charlotte greet passersby with big Chanukah smiles.

Bottom:
MYRTLE BEACH. Rabbi Doron Aizenman, director of the newly opened Chabad House in Myrtle Beach, South Carolina, lights an improvised menorah.

Ohio

Facing page:
Top:
CINCINATTI. Among those attending a special Chanukah ceremony at Mayor Charlie Luken's office are City Councilman Bortz, Rabbi Sholom B. Kalmanson, Director of the Chabad House, and Mrs. Shterna Kalmanson.
Bottom:
COLUMBUS. Rabbi Chaim Capland, director of the House of Tradition (far right), at a Tzivos Hashem Chanukah rally in front of the Jewish Community Center.
Left:
CLEVELAND. A young girl helps Rabbi Mordechai Mendelson, coordinator of Chabad campus activites in Cleveland, entertain the crowd before the candle-lighting ceremony.
Below
With his Mobile Menorah parked at a shopping center, Chaim Boruch Alevksy of Chabad House gives a Chanukah kit to a shopper.

Oregon

PORTLAND. Carrying a special torch to light the giant menorah in Pioneer Courthouse Square is Rabbi Moshe Wilhelm, flanked by Mayor Bud Clark (left) and onlookers.
Facing page:
Mayor Clark lighting the menorah on the fifth night at a special ceremony for the city's children.
Below:
The children and the Mayor gather on the Square steps, after the ceremony, for a special Chanukah rally.

Pennsylvania

PITTSBURGH. This majestic menorah, standing at the Lubavitch Yeshiva on the Heights, illuminated the highways of Pittsburgh, bringing the spirit of Chanukah to thousands.

PHILADELPHIA. The menorah at Independence Mall, as seen from the Liberty Bell, as it celebrates two hundred years from the signing of the constitution, guaranteeing religious liberty and freedom.

Facing page:
Rabbi Menachem Shmidt of the Lubavitch House in Philadelphia, lights the giant menorah outside City Hall in Dilworth Plaza, as Leonard Elkins assists.
Bottom:
The menorah at Independence Mall, opposite the Bell.

Top:
HARRISBURG. A menorah on the spot, for people on the go, made by representatives of Lubavitch in Philadelphia.
Right:
PITTSBURGH. The menorah in downtown.

HARRISBURG. Rabbi M. Hurwitz lights the menorah at the State Capitol in Harrisburg.
Bottom:
PITTSBURGH. Rabbi Sholom Posner, one of the oldest Lubavitch emmisaries in America, stands with some of his younger colleagues in front of the great menorah at the City County building.

Rhode Island

PROVIDENCE. Superior Court Judge Richard Israel, lights the menorah in the rotunda of the State House. From left: Rabbi Yehoshua Laufer, Director of Chabad activities in Rhode Island, Governor Edward DiPrete, Judge Israel and Rabbi M. Drazin of Cong. B'nai Jacob.

In commemorating 350 years of religious freedom in Rhode Island (first in freedom in the United States), Rabbi Laufer presents a special publication based on essays by the Lubavitcher Rebbe, entitled "Divine providence and the preservation of the American Ideal", to the Governor. The Governor said that he would cherish the essays and hoped to learn and live by their lessons.

Governor DiPrete and Judge Israel, stand in front of the original charter signed by King Charles II, granting religious freedom to Rhode Island.

Texas

End of Hanukkah

Rabbi Yosef Levertov, director of the Chabad House in Austin, on Friday places oil into laterns, making up a huge menorah on the University of Texas campus. Friday night was the final celebration of Hanukkah, the Jewish Festival of Light.

Facing page:

Top:
EL PASO. The newly arrived Lubavitcher representative to El Paso, Rabbi Israel Grinberg, as he prepares to bring spiritual light to the Sun City, via El Paso's first outdoor menorah.

Bottom left:
At the La-Tuna Federal Prison in El Paso.

Left:
DALLAS. Rabbi Mendel Dubrawsky, Director of Lubavitch activities in Dallas, Ft. Worth, lighting the menorah in Thanksgiving Square in downtown Dallas.

Bottom:
Some of the children at the Gala Lubavitch Chanukah Rally in Dallas.

HOUSTON. Rabbi B. Marinovsky, Director of Chabad-Lubavitch activities, at Texas Medical Center, in front of Chabad House at T.M.C.

This Mobile Menorah brought the message of Chanukah to the Houston skyline.

Rabbi Moshe Traxler of Chabad House, addresses the gathering at the public Chanukah menorah lighting ceremony. At his side is Rabbi Shimon Lazarov, Director of Chabad-Lubavitch in Texas, and Rabbi Marinovsky.

This lovely Chanukah skit was presented by the young "maccabees" of the Torah Day School-Lubavitch, in Houston.

S. ANTONIO. Forty Jewish servicemen
stationed at Lackland Air Force Base,
joined the Chabad-Lubavitch
representative in lighting the largest
menorah in S. Antonio.

Just three more candles to go and all eight candles will be lit!

Rabbi Chaim Block, Director of Lubavitch activities in San Antonio, addresses the crowd assembled to light the Chanukah menorah.

Vermont

BURLINGTON. Rabbi Yitzchok Raskin, Director of Lubavitch activities in Vermont, lights a giant menorah in Burlington's City Hall Park, as onlookers raise their eyes upwards (bottom). Everyone enjoyed the festive atmosphere at the Lubavitch Chanukah party in Burlington.

Virginia

VIRGINIA BEACH. The graceful lines of the highest menorah in North America, towering atop Mt. Trashmore, reminds thousands driving on Interstate 64 of the miracles of Chanukah.

NORFOLK. The Chabad menorah standing
tall at the Chamber of Commerce in
downtown.

Rabbi Aaron M. Margolin, Director of
Lubavitch activities in Tidewater, lights the
menorah with hurricane lamps on the windy
deck of the U.S.S. Theodore Roosevelt, at
the naval station in Norfolk.

OCEANA. A delegation from the Lubavitch center of Tidewater, was granted permission to light this menorah, on the runway of this naval airstation, bringing the spirit of Chanukah to the navy men stationed there.

NEWPORT NEWS. Rabbi Michael Gurkov, of Cong. Adas Yeshurun, lights the menorah in Coliseum Mall, as some shoppers lend a hand.

Below:
FAIRFAX. At the Chabad House, wide eyed youngsters listen intently to the story of Chanukah as told by the flickering Chanukah lights.

LANGLEY AIRFORCE BASE. Captain Mitch Ellen, kindles the Lubavitch sponsored menorah, at Langley Air Force Base.

Below:
VIENNA. Rabbi Yankel Bulua, Director of Chabad-Lubavitch activities in Northern Virginia, stands with Vienna Mayor Charles Robinson, and Martin Schor, at a Chanukah celebration in front of the Vienna Jewish Community Center.

RICHMOND. Lighting the menorah on the fifth night is Rabbi Yankel Kranz, Director of Lubavitch activities in the Virginias.

Right:
Mrs. Fay Kranz at a local Hospital, bringing Chanukah greetings and holiday cheer to the patients.

Bottom:
A lit menorah reminds motorists to kindle their own menorot, in celebration of the miracles of Chanukah.

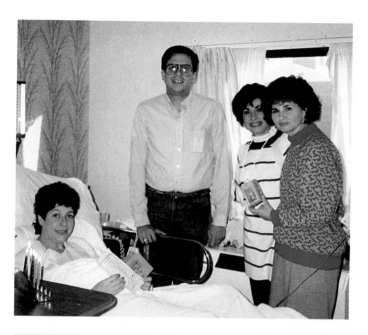

Washington

SEATTLE. The joyous spirit of Chanukah is brought to downtown Seattle, as Rabbi Yecheskiel Kornfeld of Chabad House, lights the giant menorah in Westlake Mall, and joins in a whirling chassidic dance.

Wisconsin

MILWAUKEE. More than 1,000 people attended the grand Chanukah celebration at Northridge Mall. Pictured is Mayor Henry W. Maier, addressing the assembled. The large 15-foot menorah was the first public menorah ever to be lit in Milwaukee. The boy's choir entertained with special Chanukah songs.

MADISON. The Chabad-Lubavitch Mobile Menorah wished all a "Happy Chanukah", as it visited the State Capitol.

Bottom:
KENOSHA. A Chanukah celebration with candles and Chanukah donughts, sponsored by Milwaukee Lubavitch.

MILWAUKEE. The Menorah Mobile at Milwaukee City Hall.
Bottom:
MADISON. Proud members of Tzivos Hashem pose at their Chanukah conference in Chabad House.

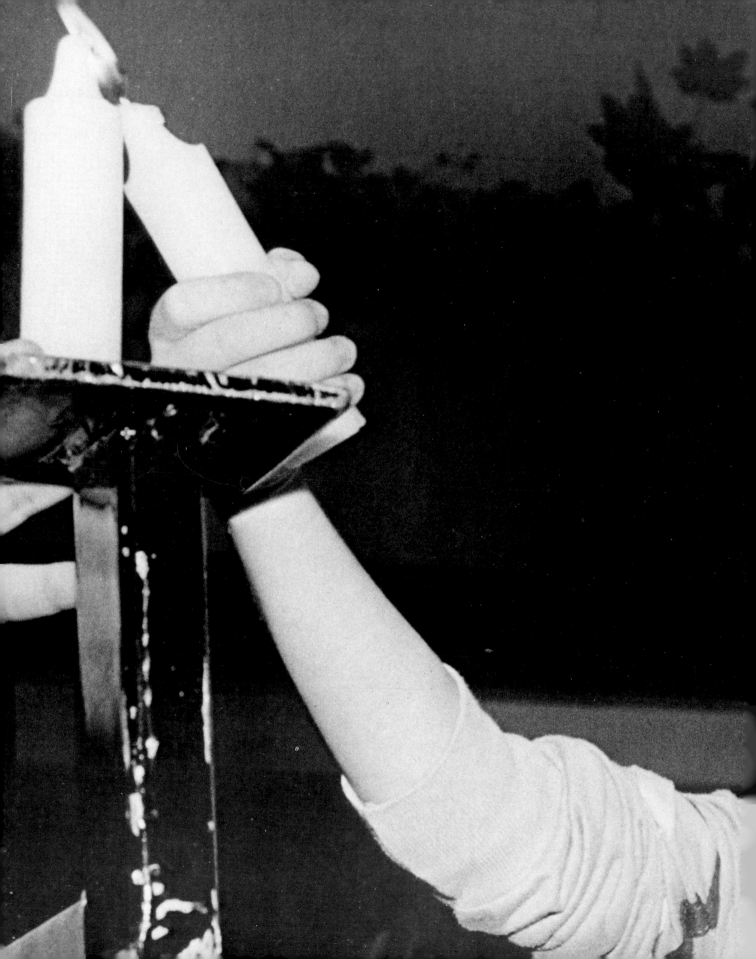

Canada

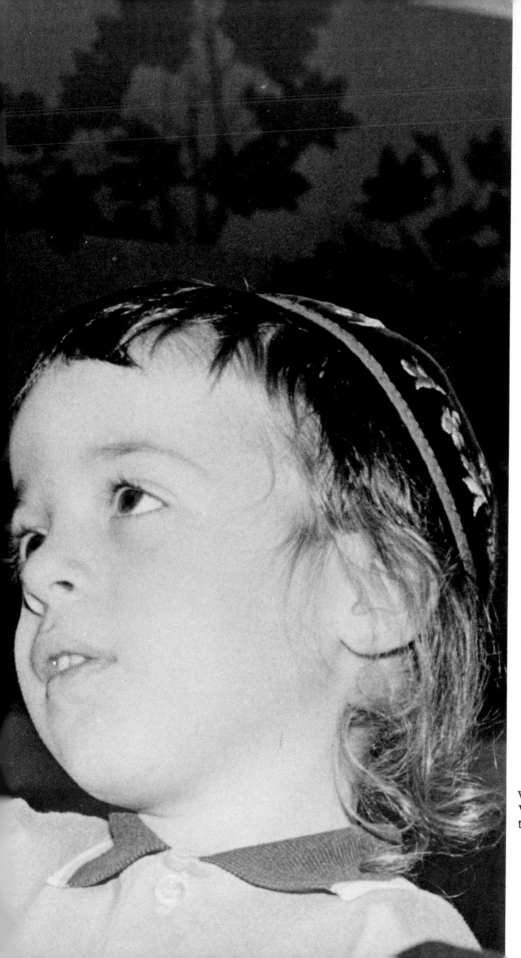

VANCOUVER, B.C. Young Avraham Varnai lights the public menorah at the Oakridge shopping center.

A festive moment as the band strikes up a lively tune, after the lighting ceremony at the Oakridge shopping center celebration (left).

VICTORIA, B.C. Rabbi Yitzchok Wineberg, Director of Chabad-Lubavitch activities in British Columbia, addresses the crowd gathered at the Parliament Building for the menorah lighting ceremony (top).

A group of lucky "Tzivos Hashem" members who attended the lighting ceremony at the Parliament (above).

RICHMOND, B.C. Rabbi Avraham
Feigelstock, of Cong. Eitz Chaim, watches as
Hillel Israel lights the menorah in Mayor Gil
Blair's office, as the Mayor looks on.

WINNIPEG, MAN. A group of campers from
"Gan Israel's" winter camp, braved the
freezing temperatures to witness the
lighting by Rabbi Yitzchok Charytan, of the
great menorah in front of Chabad House.
More than 85 children attended the camp.

MARKHAM, ONT. Rabbi Avraham Plotkin, Director of Chabad-Lubavitch activities in Markham, lights Markham's outdoor public menorah, at the intersection of Bayview Ave. and John St.

Rabbi Plotkin with Markham Councilor Michael Popovich, and York Region Councilor Ron Moran.

THORNHILL, ONT. Rabbi Zalman A. Grossbaum, Director of Chabad-Lubavitch activities in Southern Ontario, with City Councilman David Chapley and son, at the large menorah at Chabad Gate and Bathhurst St.

OTTAWA, ONT. A towering, 22-foot high, 2,000-pound menorah being erected in Confederation Park near Parliament Hill, in Canada's Capital City. From left are: Rabbi Simcha Zirkind, Lorry Greenberg, Rabbi Mordechai Berger, Morris Kimmel and Bob White.

Following pages:
Top left:
A Mobile Menorah in the Capital City, built by a group of yeshiva students from the Rabbinical College of Canada.

Bottom:
At a special Chanukah ceremony for diplomats, in the External Affairs Building, Rabbi Mordechai Berger, Director of Chabad-Lubavitch activities in Ottawa, and Aron Mayne, lead the lighting.

Right: Rabbi Berger, addresses the crowd at the community celebration in Confederation Park.

LAVAL, QUE. Rabbi Moshe New, Director of Chabad-Lubavitch activities in Laval, addresses a Chanukah Rally, in Chomedey.

MONTREAL, QUE. Hundreds were enraptured by this Chanukah play presented at the Beth Rivkah School for girls.

LAVAL. Over 250 people attended the grand Chanukah lighting ceremony of the largest Chanukah menorah in Laval, on Notre Dame St. in Chomedey. Latkes, L'Chaim and lots of dancing and one of the Mobile Menorot.

MONTREAL. A unique Chanukah program at a Montreal public school, presented by Free Hebrew for Juniors-Lubavitch.

MONTREAL. One of the many "Menorah Mobiles", which travelled the length and breadth of Montreal, bringing the Chanukah message to all.

II

Eretz Yisrael

A common sight in Israel are the "Chabad Houses On Wheels", which fan out across Israel in war and in peace. They visit farflung villages and isolated army posts. They bring joy and strength, encouragement and smiles to the forgotten soldiers on a dangerous border patrol. They give classes and audio-visual instruction to small isolated townlets in the developing areas of Israel. During war, they roll along with the Israeli tank battalions in battle after battle, raising army morale wherever they go. They are the Chabad-Lubavitch "Mitzvah Tanks."

Pictured here are the Mitzvah Tanks as they leave their base in Natzeret, on a Chanukah mission to points due North and South.

Undaunted, a Mitzvah Tank, winds its
way up a mountain pass along the
Israel-Lebanese border, with a giant
Chanukah menorah trailing.

Prime Minister Shimon Peres, lights the
menorah on a Chabad-Lubavitch
Mitzvah Tank.

"Somewhere" in Israel, a chance encounter en route to a military outpost is utilized by the Chabad "Tankists" to bring Chanukah cheer to some weary soldiers.

The maneuvers at this army camp were enhanced by a visit from the Mitzvah Tank, and by Rabbi Y. Herzel of Kfar Tavor.

General Yosef Ben-Chanan, head of the Israeli Tank corps, lights the Chabad menorah. Looking on are Rabbi Nachshon, and Rabbi Yitzchak Kogan, well-known recent emigre from the Soviet Union.

Silhouetted against the gathering dusk, an Israeli soldier illuminates a remote military base which borders Israel, Syria and Jordan.

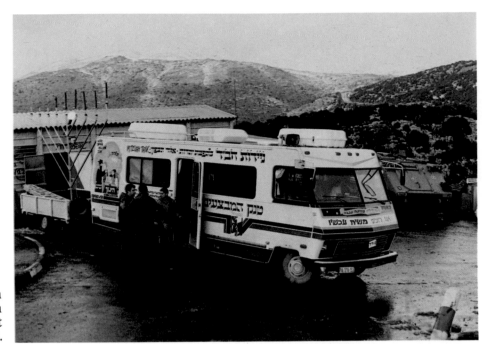

At a military observation post on the snow-capped Hermon mountain peaks, this giant menorah was seen far and wide.

With weapons at rest, a group of soldiers pause to put on *tefillin,* at a military installation in Lebanon.

This Mitzvah Tank brought a great deal of Chanukah smiles to this border settlement.

Internationally acclaimed author Herman Wouk spent a busy day aboard a Mitzvah Tank. Here a group of excited youngsters pose with Mr. Wouk and Rabbi David Nachshon, Director of the Chabad Mobile Mitzvah Centers in Israel, after hearing a special Chanukah lesson on board.

Yehuda & Shomron

The Mitzvah Tank, takes up a position at the
Western Wall.

U.N. Ambassador Benjamin Netanyahu, lights the menorah on the Chabad-Lubavitch Mitzvah Tank (right). Outside the Old City, the menorah attracts young and old (bottom).

The Mitzvah Tank at the walls of
Old Jerusalem.

KARNEI SHOMRON. A mountain-top menorah illuminates the entire Judah and Samaria.

Insets:
Left:
ARIEL. A menorah lighting ceremony in the municipal offices, with Mayor Ron Nachman, assisted by the Director of the Chabad House, Rabbi Samuel Omer.
Center:
Rabbi Omer lights the outdoor menorah.
Right:
EMANUEL. Rabbi Omer kindles the menorah, atop the tallest building in this new city.

Central Israel

Rabbi Yosef Gerlitzky, Director of Chabad Lubavitch activities in Tel Aviv, and Rabbi of central Tel Aviv, addresses a crowd of over 1,000 people, which gathered to witness the kindling of the giant menorah by Vice Mayor Nathan Wallach.

Facing Page:
HOLON. City Rabbi Yochanan Gurary, lights the giant menorah in the center of Kiryat Sharet.

Rabbi Menachem Gurewitz tells the story of Chanukah, at a rally for the children (top), and entertains the elderly at a local old age home, with some fascinating Chanukah thoughts (bottom).

Left:
NESS ZIYYONA. Mr. Manny Weizman lights the city's central
menorah.
Center:
The rally for the youngsters of "Tzivos Hashem", saw an overflow
crowd.
Right:
A little light brings much happiness to this local old age home.

ROSH HA'AYIN. The menorah which could not be missed by the
residents of this town.

MAVOH MO'DIN. This Chabad-Lubavitch menorah stood along the highway, at the entrance to this settlement.
Insets:
REHOVOT. Mayer Yecheskiel Hermlich, lights the menorah in the center of the town (top). City Chief Rabbi Simcha Kook, is honored with lighting the menorah (center). Rabbi Aryeh Levin, assists some youngsters gathered in the center of town, in lighting their own menorot.

חנוכה שמח צעירי חב"ד
מיוצר ע"י בתי ספר למלאכה כפר חב"ד

33·356·80

Facing page:
RISHON L'ZION. The Mobile Menorah stands alongside the giant menorah in the center of town.
Top:
Rabbi Gruzman conducts a children's rally in the Ganei Rishon district.
Bottom:
Bringing Chanukah to the local police station.

RAMAT HASHARON. A unique menorah seems to rise from the ground at the entrance to the city.
Insets, top:
LOD. Rising into the night to light the giant menorah.
Bottom:
HERZELIYA. A gold-gilded Mobile Menorah, manned by Rabbi Yisrael Halpern.

BAT YAM. A Mobile Menorah (facing page, top), and in the Anne Frank shopping center (bottom), a break for menorah lighting in midst of a hectic business day. A visit to the local police station (above).

Northern Israel

TIBERIAS. A unique, floating menorah on the
peaceful waters of the Kineret.

SAFSUFA. Settlement chairman, Mr. Danny Saida, lights the Chabad Communal menorah.

Rabbi Yosef Chitrik of Safed addresses a Chanukah rally for the young and old.

KIRYAT MOTZKIN. City Rabbi Chaim Drukman, kindles the large outdoor menorah.

MENAHEMIA. A commanding officer of the Border Patrol lights a menorah overlooking the Jordan Valley.

TIBERIAS. A last minute send-off with Chanukah paraphernalia, by young Chabadniks of Tiberias.
Insets:
TIRAT HAKARMEL. At the lighting of the public menorah (left), and a mini Chanukah rally in front of the Mobile Menorah (center).
Inset Right:
Israeli Chanukah "sufganiyot"–doughnuts, are handed to troops en route to their army base.

SAFED. A fleet of mobile menorot setting out to illuminate the upper Galilee.
Facing Page, top:
Rabbi Baruch Lepkefker and Rabbi Yosef Chitrik, help the chief of police, Mr. Menachem Yosef, in putting on *tefillin*.
Bottom:
RAMAT YISHAI. City Rabbi Yosef Y. Wolosow, lights the menorah in the center of town.

MIGDAL HA'EMEK. Lighting the outdoor
menorah (left), and before an overflow
crowd at the Grand Chanukah Rally, in
Migdal Ha'emek (below).

Following Pages:
HAIFA. This menorah, on a Haifa university
rooftop, atop Mt. Carmel, was seen
throughout northern Israel.
Insets:
Dancing around the menorah at Masrik
Plaza, on the second night of Chanukah
(left), City Ashkenazi Chief Rabbi Sha'er
Yashov, with assistance from Director of
Chabad activities in Haifa, Rabbi Laibel
Shildkraut, lights the menorah in the
Panorama shopping mall (center), City
Sefardi Chief Rabbi Bakshi Doron, lights the
menorah (right).

NAZERET EILIT. In the center of town, this menorah is lit via cherry-picker on the seventh night of Chanukah.

B'NAI AYASH. Sponsored by Chabad of Gedeva, this Chanukah rally attracted 150 children.

YESOD HA'MALEH. City Rabbi Yaakov Raices, with a group of children from Tzivos Hashem, gathered for a Chanukah party at the "Chabad House."

AFULA. No need for a ladder here, they
have their own "patent" (above). A young
soldier in Tzivos Hashem, reciting the
twelve well-known Torah passages (right).

NAHARIYA. Lighting the menorah at the
Municipal Building in the center of the city
(facing page). Rabbi Yisroel Baruch
Butman, Director of Chabad-Lubavitch
activities in Nahariya, addressing family
members of the police force (inset).

AKO. Mayor Eli DeCastro was given the honors, on the second night of Chanukah.

Facing Page—top:
KIRYAT TIV'ON. City Councilman Mr. David Maron, reciting the blessings before lighting the menorah.

Bottom:
LOWER GALILEE. Bringing the warmth of Chanukah to the soldiers at an army base is Rabbi Yehoshua Herzel of Kfar Tavor.

Southern Israel

At a military training camp for officers in the sun drenched Negev, rabbinical student Moshe Heber, brings the Chanukah message of "the few over the many", to members of the Israel Defense Forces.

KIRYAT GAT. The center of
town was home for this giant
menorah.

ARAD. Rabbi Levi Yitzchak
Raskin, Director of
Chabad-Lubavitch activities
in Arad, assisting the Mayor,
Mr. Avraham Schochet, in
lighting the menorah.

ASHKELON. One thousand people
witnessed Ashkelon Mayor Eli
Dayan, light the menorah in the
center of the city.

EILAT. Proclaiming Chanukah from the
rooftops—and what better location than
the center of the city.

Mayor Raphael Hochman lighting the rooftop menorah. From left: Rabbi Yisroel Glitzenstein, local Director of Lubavitch Youth Organization and his colleague Rabbi Baruch Lepkefker.

Eilat Rabbi Yosef Hecht, lighting the menorah at the Eilat Tourist Center. This menorah could be seen from the Jordanian port city of Aqaba (background).

A job well done! The Chabad Mitzvah Tanks making their way back to base, after bringing the festive Chanukah spirit to thousands.

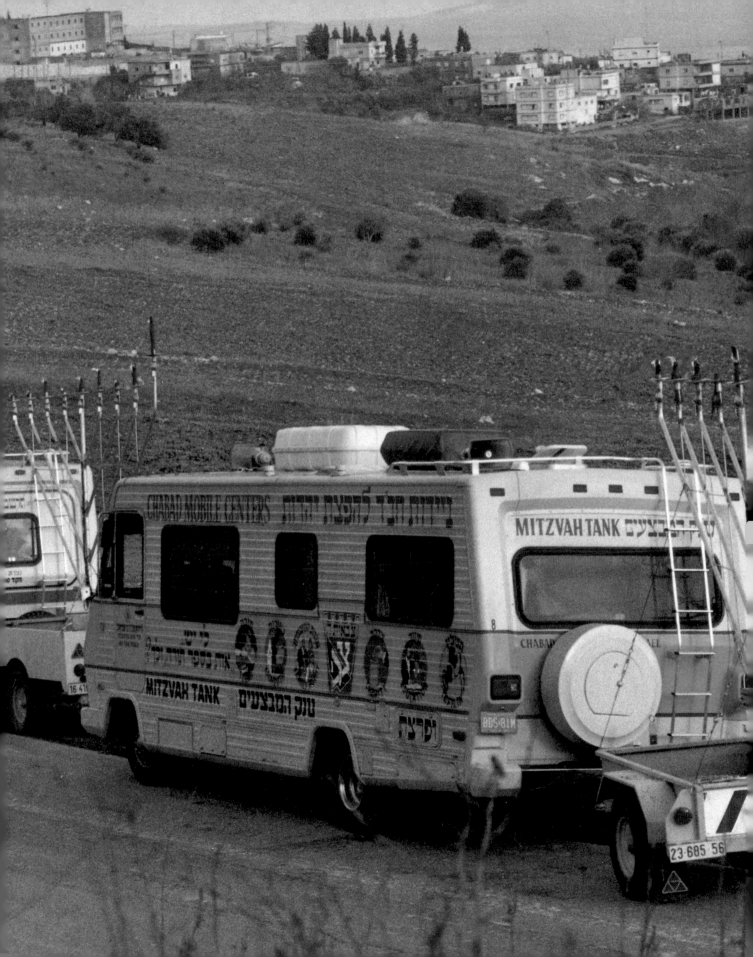

III
Africa

MOROCCO
SOUTH AFRICA
TUNISIA

Morocco

BEN ACHMED. Rabbi Yehuda Leib Raskin, Director of Chabad-Lubavitch activities in North Africa, in a visit to a local synagogue, brings some of the Chanukah spirit to fellow Jews.

Facing page, top:
CASABLANCA. These Morrocon children seem to be having a great time, as they sing and clap at the grand Chanukah celebration held at the Lubavitch Center.
Bottom:
MEKNES. Lubavitch of Morroco has not forgotten the Jewish children of Meknes, where this festive Chanukah celebration took place.

CASABLANCA. The portrait of King Hassan seems to be smiling at the Chanukah joy, brought by Rabbi Raskin to the Alliance Club.

South Africa

JOHANNESBURG. A giant 13-foot menorah attracted thousands of spectators at Killarney Mall Shopping Centre. Each evening saw a different guest speaker and cantor officiate, followed by live music and dancing.

KILLARNEY MALL AND THE LUBAVITCH FOUNDATION WISH THE JEWISH COMMUNITY A HAPPY CHANUKAH בה נבהש נ.ג.ה.ש

At the celebration, from left: South African Chief Rabbi B.M. Casper; Rabbi Mendel Lipskar, Director of Chabad-Lubavitch activities in South Africa; Johannesburg Mayor Professor H. Rudolph. Lighting the menorah is Cantor Dvir.

CAPE TOWN. A group of South
African children look on in
wonder as Cape Town Mayor
Leon Markovitz lights the huge
Chabad menorah. Assisting the
mayor is Rabbi Mendel Popack,
Director of Lubavitch activities
in the Cape area.

Tunisia

TUNIS. A shining combination—glowing Chanukah candles and young smiling faces, enjoying the holiday of Chanukah. Directing the get-together in this isolated Jewish community are Rabbi and Mrs. Nissan Pinson, Directors of Chabad-Lubavitch activities in Tunisia.

IV
Australia
& Hong Kong

Australia

MELBOURNE. The Chabad-Lubavitch menorah at City Square, with the Melbourne Town Hall in the background.

MELBOURNE. Attracting a crowd is the
Chabad Mobile Centre, flanked by a junior
mobile unit.

The ceremony at the City Square menorah is about to begin.

The spirit of Chanukah was also brought to far-flung Jewish communities 'down under.' In Southern Australia, Adelaide Synagogue was the venue for this celebration (top). Sydney Rabbinical students Sholom Rosenfeld and Sholom Paltiel brought Chanukah joy to Launceston, Tasmania (right).
Facing page.
Rabbinical student Yossie Lipsker lights a menorah in the center of Brisbane, the capital of Queensland (top); while in the Australian capital of Canberra, Israeli Ambassador Yissachar Ben-Yaakov was honored with kindling the large outdoor menorah.

MITZVAH CAMPAIGN

DIAL A JEWISH STORY 527 5037

AHAVAT YISROEL
TO LOVE A FELLOW JEW

CHINUCH
TORAH EDUCATION

TORAH STUDY
EVERY DAY EVERY NIGHT

TEFILLIN
THE DONNING OF TEFILLIN EVERY
WEEKDAY BY MEN & BOYS OVER 13 YEARS

MEZUZAH
THE JEWISH SIGN

TZEDOKAH
GIVING CHARITY EVERY WEEKDAY

POSSESSION
OF JEWISH HOLY BOOKS

NESHEK
LIGHTING OF SHABBAT & FESTIVAL CANDLE

KASHRUT
JEWISH DIETARY LAWS

TAHARAT HAMISHPACHA
THE TORAH PERSPECTIVE ON MARRIED LIFE

SEFER TORAH
UNITING THE JEWISH PEOPLE

St. Kilda Signs

MELBOURNE. The Chabad Mitzvah Mobile Centre on Hotham Street (far left). SYDNEY. Rabbi Pinchas Feldman, Director of Chabad-Lubavitch in Sydney, lights the large menorah (left).

The campers at Sydney's Chabad-Lubavitch summer camp not only lit their own menorot they also designed and constructed them.

Hong Kong

The newly arrived Chabad-Lubavitch representatives to Hong Kong, Rabbi & Mrs. Mordechai Avtzon, erected the Territory's first outdoor menorah. The menorah in Chater Garden Central stood 12 feet tall and was made of solid brass. The event was widely covered by the press, including this article which appeared in the Chinese daily *Sing Pao*.

具二千年歷史猶太節日

燭光祭昨舉行

願樂觀與希望普照人間

【本報特訊】一個已有兩千年歷史的猶太節日，昨八七年元旦首次在港舉行，該個名為「燭光祭」節日，原意是「燭光祭」在港舉行，更具意義。

昨晚七時，為數約七十名居港猶太裔人士及少量中外人士，齊集在中區遮打公園，圍繞一支圖案式樹形燈柱舉行「燭光祭」，該燈柱柱頂綴一燈膽，柱身兩邊各伸出四條柱枝，枝末各綴一燈膽。儀式開始在場觀禮小朋友上前，一同將燭台上蠟燭點燃，主禮者隨即致詞表示：希望燭光燃亮每人心

相同燭台，只是燭台上中其中一個燭座並未放上蠟燭。

主禮者致詞歡迎及祝福各人後，首先按電掣點亮燈柱上八個燈膽的其中七個，然後再召集在場觀禮小朋友上前，其中頂部燈則放置一具與燈柱形狀，燈柱台座一角膽亮着，燈柱正中頂部燈

◇（上）數十猶太人在「希望之光」前舉行「燭光祭」。（下）儀式舉行後主禮者派利是。

V
Europe

England

LONDON. Big Ben was no match for the menorah, which swiftly became the center of attraction.

UBAVITCH WISHES YOU A HAPPY CHANUKAH
WE WANT MOSHIACH NOW !
EPL International
PLANT AND ACCESS HIRE
Happy Chanukah from...
JEWISH HERALD
LONDONS OWN JEWISH NEWSPAPER
Happy Chanukah from...
JEWISH HERALD
LONDONS OWN JEWISH NEWSPAPER

Facing Page:
LONDON. The menorah in Golders Green says it all.

This Page:
LEEDS. This was Europe's first giant menorah (Chanukah 5743/1983).

From Left To Right: Stephen Forman (Chairman Leeds Jewish Youth Council), Rabbi Reuven Cohen (Youth Director-Leeds Lubavitch), and Yaacov Laher.

MANCHESTER. The menorah at Albert Square, is kindled by Rabbi Michoel Cohen of Manchester Lubavitch, and Mr. Henry Gutterman.

The Albert Square menorah proudly
aglow in front of Manchester's Town Hall.

France

PARIS. Hundreds of giant billboards, like this one, reminded the citizens of the 'city of lights,' of the upcoming Festival of Lights.

50079 G
PUISSANCE 7
AVENIR
ALLUMEZ VOS BOUGIES !
au 2/1/87
Du 26/12/86
'HANOUCCAH
1986
BETH LOUBAVITCH - PARIS

GRENOBLE. In the Menorah Mobile, a
lively discussion with Rabbi E.
Lahayani, Director of Chabad-
Lubavitch activities in Grenoble.
Below:
METZ-NANCY. Rabbi Yehuda Leib
Matusof, Director of Chabad-
Lubavitch activities in Metz-Nancy,
leading an informal Chanukah
get-together.

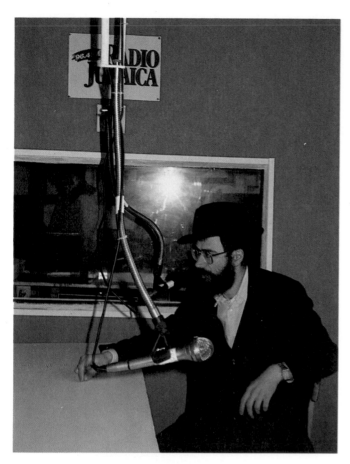

LILLE. Rabbi Eli Dahan conducting a special Chanukah program on French radio.

Below:
TOULOUSE. Bringing Chanukah to the City Hall Capitole.

Giant electronic billboards, like these in Grenoble and Nice, announced the daily schedule for lighting the menorah.

ville de grenoble
informations

LA JEUNESSE
LOUBAVITCH VOUS
SOUHAITE UN JOYEUX
** HANOUCCA **
ALLUMAGE DES
8 BOUGIES VEN 2/0
AVANT 16H30

e
rmations
LA JEUNESSE
UBAVITCH VOUS
HAITE UNE BONNE
E DE HANNOUCA &
PELLE DIMANCHE
18H : ALLUMAGE
DE 8 BOUGIES

PARIS. Kindling the Chanukah lights in the streets of the French capital (left); and a Chanukah rally at one of the largest Parisian theatres, saw an overflow crowd of more than 1300 children.

SARCELLES. The Menorah Mobile
on the highway.

Italy

MILAN. A reminder to Italian Jews to kindle their own
menorah's during the festival of Chanukah.
Facing page:
CAMAIORE. Yeshivah students from Milan brought some
Chanukah joy to this resort town in northern Italy, when
they lit a menorah in front of the Town Hall.

(On the poster:)

CHANUCCA'

DA VENERDI' SERA
OTTO GIORNI DI LUCE,
DI PACE, NELLE NOSTRE
CASE, NEL MONDO.

IL PRIMO LUME SI ACCENDE ENTRO LE 16,25

MERKOS L'INYONEI CHINUCH

PADOVA. Rabbi Eli D. Borenstein, Director of Chabad-Lubavitch activities in Bologna, leads an informal Chanukah celebration.
Below:
BOLOGNA. The honorable Mr. De Paz, at the menorah lighting ceremony in the center of the city.

ROME. This menorah was lit in one of the stores in the "Jewish Ghetto" of Rome.
Below:
LADISPOLI. Rabbi Yitzchak Chazan, Director of Chabad-Lubavitch activities in Rome, was the guest speaker at a Chanukah celebration held at the Chabad House, which is under the direction of Rabbi H. Bisk (seated at the head of the table).

Spain

Facing page:
MADRID. This Mobile Menorah brought the joy of Chanukah to the Jews in Spain.

Top:
TOLEDO. Rabbi Yitzchok Goldstein, Director of Chabad-Lubavitch activities in Spain, lit a large menorah in front of Toledo's ancient Transito Synagogue, in what was the first public Jewish ceremony held in that city since the expulsion of the Jews in 1492. The event captured the interest of national and international press, giving the story wide coverage. "One mitzvah leads to another," as Rabbi Goldstein helped several men put on *tefillin.*

Bottom:
MASSADA. At a Chanukah outing outside Madrid, Yossi Benharosh and Sammy Bensadon, pose with their children, by the largest Chanukah menorah they have ever seen.

Switzerland

ZURICH. "Educate the child according to his way." A father assists his son at a Chanukah celebration at the Chabad House.
Below:
In the center of town, at the Paradeplatz, this menorah brought the Chanukah festival to Jews in Zurich.

ZURICH. A little girl gets a helping hand with her candles.
Below:
Outside the Lubavitch Center.

Austria · Belgium · Scotland

VIENNA. A Chanukah rally for Jewish children.

ANTWERP. Music, song, smiles and spontaneous dancing were all part of the Chanukah celebration at the local Chabad House; while uniformed "soldiers" of Tzivos Hashem, study the words of Torah.

GLASGOW. Rabbi Adrian Jesner lights the menorah at Glasgow Macabbi, as Rabbi Chaim Jacobs, Director of Chabad-Lubavitch activities in Scotland and Mr. Allan, look on.

VI

South America

ARGENTINA
BRAZIL
CHILE
COLOMBIA
PANAMA
URUGUAY
VENEZUELA

Argentina

BUENOS AIRES.
As the sun sets
over the capital
city, the uniquely
decorated menorah,
the largest in
Argentina, is
readied for lighting.

Previous page:
Top:
In an act of Jewish unity the Jews of Buenos Aires gathered by the thousands
to celebrate Chanukah in a downtown plaza.
Bottom left and below:
Jewish communal leaders and members of the Argentine Congress watch as
Dr. David Goldberg, president of the D.A.I.A. delegation to the government, and
Israeli ambassador Dr. Efraim Tari, light the menorah.

BAHIA BLANCA. As all eight lights were kindled on the last night of Chanukah, this giant menorah was the talk of the town. Rabbi Moshe Freedman, Director of Lubavitch activities in Bahia Blanca, assists Mr. Yaakov Pallevik with the Chanukah blessings.

CONCORDIA. Rabbi Y. Kapeluchnik, of Concordia Lubavitch, lights the local Mobile Menorah.

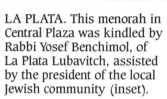

LA PLATA. This menorah in
Central Plaza was kindled by
Rabbi Yosef Benchimol, of
La Plata Lubavitch, assisted
by the president of the local
Jewish community (inset).

MIRAMAR. Chanukah was not
forgotten in this resort city, thanks
to the efforts of Lubavitch of
Argentina.

TUCUMAN. At a special Chanukah
celebration, which took place in the
streets of the city, are Rabbi D. Levy,
Director of Lubavitch activities
in Tucuman (far left) and
Mr. Marcos Najlis.

Brazil

S. PAULO. This majestic menorah has a most unique home,—"Mashiach Now Square," which was dedicated by the city of S. Paulo, to the Lubavitcher Rebbe.

Facing Page:
The official military police orchestra adding to the Chanukah festivities, as
Dr. David Roysen lights the menorah in "Mashiach Now Square."

CURITIBA. Over 500 people attended the inauguration of a majestic menorah in the center of town. The event was covered by all the local newspapers and TV stations. Honored with lighting the menorah was the President of the Jewish Federation (speaking). Seated, second from right, is Rabbi Yosef Dubrawsky, Director of Chabad-Lubavitch activities in Curitiba.

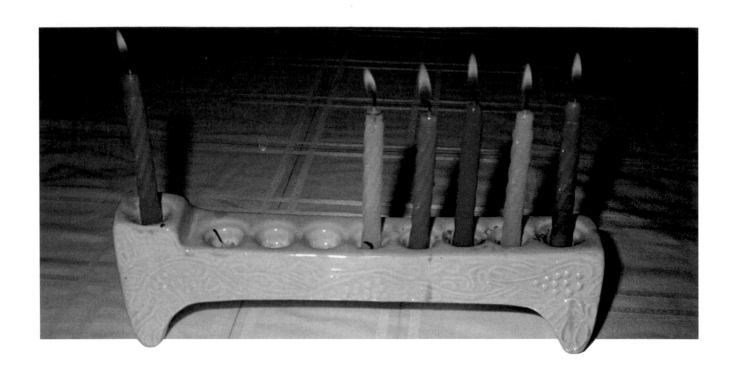

Facing Page:
CURITIBA. Beautiful menorahs such as this one, were distributed to thousands of Jews in many cities of Brazil. They were manufactured by a friend of Lubavitch, who owns a ceramic factory in Curitiba.

Bottom Left:
BELEM. These youngsters attended a Chanukah rally for members of Tzivos Hashem, which took place at the Chabad House.

Bottom Right:
BELO HORIZONTE. Menorah lighting ceremony at a Chanukah get-together for the Jewish community at Chabad House.

Left:
PORTO ALEGRE. The first public Chanukah lighting ceremony, in Porto Alegre was attended by a large group of proud and enthusiastic Jews, who danced in the streets celebrating their own small miracle of having a public menorah of their own. Present were the mayor, high ranking ministers and a special representative from the governor. The event was covered by local press and TV. Rabbi Mendel Lieberow, Director of Chabad Lubavitch activities in Porto Alegro, addressed the crowd.

ATIBAIA. The "Grande Festa De Chanuka", in the presence of the Mayor, brought nothing but smiles to the Jews of this small remote city. Rabbis Dovid Weitman and Yossi Schildkrant of Chabad House in S. Paulo, visited various outlying communities with a Mobile Menorah.

The Mobile Menorah reached out to the resort island of Guaruja, bringing the joy of Chanukah to even more Brazilian Jews.

RECIFE. Rabbi Yaakov Chazan, Director of Chabad-Lubavitch activities in Recife, is seen here with Dr. Marco Maciel, chief-of-staff to the President of Brazil, who visited the Chabad center and was present at the menorah lighting ceremony. Dr. Maciel subsequently sent a special message from the President to the Lubavitcher Rebbe, in honor of the Rebbe's 85th birthday. Left is Brazilian Congressman Dr. Pedro Correia Neto.

The public menorah that brought light and joy to the Jews of Recife.

S. PAULO. These youngsters at the Jewish Club, had all their Chanukah needs taken care of by the Lubavitch Youth Organization—*dreidels,* menorahs, Chanukah *Gelt,* and Chanukah booklets. . .the smiles, however, were purely their own (bottom).

Facing Page:
The monthly journal *Chabad,* published by Chabad-Lubavitch of S. Paulo, boasts a readership of over 12,000, in Brazil, Portugal and other Portuguese speaking countries. The cover of the Chanukah edition shows the National Menorah at Lafayette Park, in Washington D.C.

ב"ה
Chabad
ENCICLOPÉDIA MENSAL DO JUDAÍSMO
A LUZ
VARRE
AS TREVAS

Chile

SANTIAGO. Camera. . . Chanukah lights. . . ACTION! All eyes are focused on
the giant Chanukah menorah at Kennedy Plaza, which illuminated this South
American country. Rabbi Menashe Perman, Director of Chabad Lubavitch
activities in Chile, and Mr. David Fuerstein conducted the celebration.

Colombia

BOGOTA. Addressing the crowd at the menorah lighting ceremony at the "Monumento a los Heros Plaza," are: Rabbi Yehoshua B. Rosenfeld, Director of Chabad-Lubavitch activities in Colombia; and Bogota Government Secretary Dr. Bula Camache.

Facing page:
At a Chanukah gathering in Chabad House for the elderly, a solo of favorite Chanukah songs.

Panama • Uruguay

Top:
MONTEVIDEO. From left to right, at the Chabad-Lubavitch menorah: Mr. Roberto Wajner, President of Kehila Israelita Del Uruguay; Dr. Jorge Luis Elizalde, Mayor of Montevideo; Mr. Nelson Canias, President of Kehila Sefaradi; and Rabbi Eliezer Shemtov, Director of Centro Lubavitch of Uruguay.

Bottom:
PANAMA. Rabbi Zushe Wilhelm, brings Chanukah greetings to fellow Jews in Panama.

CARACAS. This Mobile Menorah wished everyone "Feliz Januca!"

Chabad-Lubavitch Spans the Globe

Lubavitch World Headquarters
770 Eastern Parkway
Brooklyn, New York 11213
718-493-9250
718-774-4000

United States of America

Alabama

Chabad House
2025 University Boulevard
Birmingham, AL 35233
205-328-6724

Chabad House
2358 Fairlane Drive #H-75
Montgomery, AL 36116
205-277-2666

Arizona

Chabad-Lubavitch
1536 E. Maryland
Phoenix, AZ 85014
602-274-5377

Chabad of Tri City
23 W. 9th Street
Tempe, AZ 85281
602-966-5163

Chabad-Lubavitch
1301 E. Elm
Tucson, AZ 85719
602-881-7955

California

Chabad of Agoura
368 N. Kanan Road
Agoura Hills, CA 91301
818-991-0991

Chabad of Anaheim
518 S. Brookhurst
Anaheim, CA 92804
714-520-0770

Chabad House
2340 Piedmont Avenue
Berkeley, CA 94704
415-540-5824

Chabad of North Beverly Hills
409 N. Foothill
Beverly Hills, CA 90210
213-859-3948

Chabad of Brentwood
11836 S. Vincente Boulevard
#208
Brentwood, CA 90049
213-471-4594

Chabad of the Valley
4915 Hayvenhurst
Encino, CA 91436
818-784-9985

Chabad of West Orange County
5702 Clark Drive #18
Huntington Beach, CA 92649
714-846-2285

Chabad Jewish Center
4872 Royce Road
Irvine, CA 92715
714-786-5000

Chabad of La Jolla
8950 Via La Jolla Drive #25
La Jolla, CA 92037
619-455-1670

Chabad of Laguna
2764 Highland Way
Laguna Beach, CA 92651
714-494-4282

Chabad of South Bay
24412 Narbonne Avenue
Lomita, CA 90717
213-326-8234

Congregation Lubavitch
3981 Atlantic Avenue
Long Beach, CA 91807
213-434-6338

Chabad-Lubavitch
101 N. Edinburgh Avenue
Los Angeles, CA 90048
213-931-0913

Chabad House
741 Gayley Avenue
Los Angeles, CA 90024
213-208-7511

Chabad Russian Center
221 S. La Brea Avenue
Los Angeles, CA 90036
213-938-1837

Chabad Mid-City Center
420 N. Fairfax Avenue
Los Angeles, CA 90036
213-655-9282

Chabad Israeli Center
9017 W. Pico Boulevard
Los Angeles, CA 90035
213-271-6193

Ohr Elchanan Chabad
7215 Waring Avenue
Los Angeles, CA 90046
213-937-3763

Chabad of Cheviot Hills
3355 Manning Avenue
Los Angeles, CA 90064
213-837-4941

Chabad Ohel Yosef Yitzchok
1925 N. Fairfax Avenue
Los Angeles, CA 90036
213-650-4765

Chabad Drug Rehabilitation
1952 Robertson Boulevard
Los Angeles, CA 90034
213-204-3196

Chabad Russian Outreach Program
7414 S. Monica Boulevard
Los Angeles, CA 90046
213-874-7583

Chabad of the Marina
13221-D Admiral Drive
Marina Del Ray, CA 90292
213-305-7469

Chabad House
425 Avienda Ortega
Palm Springs, CA 92264
619-325-0774

Chabad of the Peninsula
3070 Louis Road
Palo Alto, CA 94303
415-424-9800

Chabad of Palos Verdes
777 Silver Spur Road #128
Rolling Hills Estate, CA 90274
213-544-5544

Chabad House
6115 Montezuma Road
S Diego, CA 92115
619-265-7700

Chabad House of S. Monica
1428 17th Street
S Monica, CA 90404
213-829-5620

Chabad of Marin
POB 13871
S Rafael, CA 94913
415-492-1666

Blauner Youth Center
18211 Burbank Boulevard
Tarzana, CA 92356
818-881-2352

Reisboro Educational Center
18141 Burbank Boulevard
Tarzana, CA 91356
818-344-7142

Chabad House
13079 Chandler Boulevard
Van Nuys, CA 91401
818-989-9539

Chabad of Conejo
741 Lakefield Road #8
Westlake Village, CA 91361
818-991-0991

Hebrew Academy
14401 Willow Lane
Westminster, CA 92683
213-596-1681

Colorado

Chabad House
3100 Arapahoe
Boulder, CO 80303
303-440-7772

Chabad-Lubavitch
3465 Nonchalant Circle East
Colorado Springs, CO 80917
303-596-7330

Chabad-Lubavitch
400 S. Holly Street
Denver, CO 80222
303-329-0211

Chabad House
904 E. Elizabeth Street
Fort Collins, CO 80524
303-484-9971

Connecticut

Chabad of Greater New Haven
566 Whalley Avenue #1B
New Haven, CT 06511
203-397-1111

New Haven Hebrew Day School
261 Derby Avenue
Orange, CT 06477
203-795-5261

Chabad-Lubavitch
77 Mount Pleasant Drive
Trumbull, CT 06611
203-268-7700

Chabad House
798 Farmington Avenue
West Hartford, CT 06119
203-233-5912

Delaware

Chabad-Lubavitch
903-C Cloister Road
Wilmington, DE 19809
302-798-9151

Florida

Chabad-Lubavitch
19146 Lyons Road
Century Village West
Boca Raton, FL
305-344-2778

Chabad
9791 Sample Road
Coral Springs, FL 33065
305-344-2778

Congregation Levi Yitzchok Lubavitch
1295 E. Hallandale Beach Boulevard
Hallandale, FL 33009
305-458-1877

Synagogue of Inverary Lubavitch
4561 N. University Drive
Lauderhill, FL 33321
305-748-1777

Chabad of Greater Orlando
642 Green Meadow Avenue
Maitland, FL 32751
305-332-7906

Merkos-Lubavitch of Florida
1140 Alton Road
Miami Beach, FL 33139
305-673-5664

Chabad of North Dade
2590 N.E. 202 Street
North Miami Beach, FL 33180
305-932-7770

Chabad of Sarasota
2886-C Ringling Boulevard
Sarasota, FL 34237
813-955-1447

Chabad-Lubavitch
13156-A N. Dale Mabry
Tampa, FL 33618
813-963-2317

Chabad House of U.S.F.
5202 Seneca Avenue
Tampa, FL 33617
813-980-0942

Chabad of Palm Beach
1867 N. Congress Avenue
West Palm Beach, FL 33401

Georgia

Chabad-Lubavitch
5065 High Point Road
Atlanta, GA 30342
404-843-2464

Hawaii

Chabad of Hawaii
4851 Kahala Avenue
Honolulu, HI 96816
808-735-8161

Illinois

F.R.E.E.
6335 N. California
Chicago, IL 60659
312-274-5123

Lubavitch of Illinois
3107 W. Devon Avenue
Chicago, IL 60659
312-262-2770

Chabad of the Loop
401 S. Lasalle Street #770
Chicago, IL 60605
312-427-7770

Cheder Lubavitch
3635 W. Devon
Chicago, IL 60659
312-463-0663

Chabad of Niles
9263 Hamlin
Des Plaines, IL 60616
312-296-1770

Chabad House
2014 Orrington
Evanston, IL 60201
312-869-8060

North Suburban Chabad
1871 Sheahen Court
Highland Park, IL 60035
312-433-1567

Chabad House
4059 Dempster
Skokie, IL 60076
312-677-1770

Indiana

Lubavitch of Indiana
1037 Golf Lane
Indianapolis, IN 46260
317-251-5573

Iowa

Chabad of Iowa
2932 University Avenue
Des Moines, IA 50311
515-277-0770

Kentucky

Chabad-Lubavitch
2607 Landor Avenue
Louisville, KY 40205
502-459-1770

Louisiana

Chabad House
7037 Freret Street
New Orleans, LA 70118
504-866-5164

Maine

Chabad-Lubavitch
108 Noyes Street
Portland, ME 04103
207-871-8947

Maryland

Lubavitch of Maryland
3505 Pikney Road
Baltimore, MD 21215
301-340-6858

Chabad House
9650 Santiago Road
Columbia, MD 21045
301-740-2424

Chabad House
6711 Wells Parkway
Hyattsville, MD 20872
301-422-6200

Chabad House
311 W. Montgomery Avenue
Rockville, MD 20850
301-340-6858

Massachusetts

Chabad House
30 N. Hadley Road
Amherst, MA 01002
413-549-4094

Chabad House
491 Commonwealth Avenue
Boston, MA 02215
617-424-1190

Lubavitch Yeshiva
9 Prescott Street
Brookline, MA 02146
617-731-5330

Chabad House
74 Joseph Road
Framingham, MA 01701
617-877-8888

Chabad Center
9 Burlington Street
Lexington, MA 02173
617-863-8656

Yeshiva Achei Tmimim
1148 Converse Street
Longmeadow, MA 01106
413-567-8665

Shaloh House
68 Smith Road
Milton, MA 02186
617-333-0477

Chabad House
782 Dickinson
Springfield, MA 01108
413-736-3936

Yeshiva Achei Tmimim
22 Newton Avenue
Worcester, MA 01602
617-752-0904

Chabad House–Lubavitch
630 Pleasant
Worcester, MA 01602
617-754-6221

Michigan

Chabad House
715 Hill Street
Ann Arbor, MI 48104
313-769-3078

Beis Chabad
32000 Middlebelt Road
Farmington Hills, MI 48018
313-626-3194

Chabad Lubavitch of Michigan
28555 Middlebelt Road
Farmington Hills, MI 48018
313-737-7000

Chabad House
5394 Oaktree Drive
Flint, MI 48504
313-733-3779

Chabad House
2615 Michigan N.E.
Grand Rapids, MI 49506
616-458-6575

Chabad House
5595 W. Maple Road
West Bloomfield, MI 48033
313-855-6170

Minnesota

Chabad House
15 Montcalm Court
S Paul, MN 55116
612-698-3858

Missouri

Chabad House
8901 Holmes Street
Kansas City, MO 64131
816-333-7117

Chabad-Lubavitch
921 Gay Avenue
S Louis, MO 63130
314-863-3516

Nebraska

Chabad House
640 S. 124th Avenue
Omaha, NE 68154
402-330-7400

New Jersey

Friends of Lubavitch
409 Grand Avenue #7
Englewood, NJ 07631
201-568-9423

Chabad of West Monmouth
889 Old Queens Boulevard
Manalapan, NJ 07726
201-446-2701

Chabad House
POB 3366
Margate, NJ 08402
609-345-1946

Rabbinical College of America
226 Sussex Avenue
Morristown, NJ 07960
201-267-9404

Chabad House
8 Sicard Street
New Brunswick, NJ 08901
201-828-7374

Chabad House
Princeton, NJ

Chabad House of Woodcliffe
28 Douglas Terrace
Woodcliffe, NJ 07675
201-381-8008

New York

Chabad House
122 S. Main Avenue
Albany, NY 12208
518-482-5781

Chabad of Binghamton
1004 Murray Hill Road
Binghamton, NY 13903
607-797-0015

Lubavitch Youth Organization
770 Eastern Parkway
Brooklyn, NY 11213
718-953-1000

Lubavitch of East Long Island
74 Hauppauge Road
Commack, NY 11725
516-462-6640

Lubavitch of the East End
6 Hyde Lane
Coram, NY 11727
516-732-1676

Chabad House
109 Elsmere
Delmar, NY 12054
518-439-8280

Chabad House
150-02 78th Road
Flushing, NY 11367
718-591-4130

Chabad House
2501 N. Forest Road
Getzville, NY 14068
716-688-1642

N.C.F.J.E. of Nassau County
Old Country Rd/New South Rd
Hicksville, NY 11801
516-935-3636

Chabad House
902 Triphammer Road
Ithaca, NY 14850
607-257-7379

N.C.F.J.E. of Nassau County
153 E. Beach Street
Long Beach, NY 11561
516-935-3636

Chabad House
4 Phylis Terrace
Monsey, NY 10952

Chabad Education Center
216 Congers Road
New City, NY 10956
914-634-0951

Chabad-Lubavitch
310 W. 103rd Street
New York, NY 10025
212-864-5010

Chabad at NYU
C/O JCF RM. 715
566 La Guardia
New York, NY 10012
212-925-8910

Lubavitch–Mid Hudson Valley
22 Lown Court
Poughkeepsie, NY 12603
914-454-1816

Chabad-Lubavitch
36 Lattimore Road
Rochester, NY 14620
716-244-4324

Chabad of Stonybrook
2 Kenswick
Stonybrook, NY 11790
516-689-2398

Chabad Lubavitch
113 Berkeley Drive
Syracuse, NY 13210
315-424-0363

Troy Chabad Center
2306 15th Street
Troy, NY 12180
518-274-5572

Lubavitch of Westchester
5 Albermarle Road
White Plains, NY 10605
914-686-0725

Chabad of the Catskills
POB 5
Woodridge, NY 12789
914-434-8981

North Carolina

Chabad-Lubavitch
6500 Newhall Road
Charlotte, NC 28226
704-366-3984

Ohio

Chabad House
1636 Summit Road
Cincinnati, OH 45237
513-821-5100

1542 Beaverton Avenue
Cincinnati, OH 45237
513-761-5200

Chabad House
2004 S. Green Road
Cleveland, OH 44121
216-382-5050

Chabad on Campus
3392 Desota Avenue
Cleveland, OH 44118
216-371-3679

Congregation Tzemach Tzedek
1922 Lee Road
Cleveland, OH 44118
216-321-5169

Chabad House of Tradition
57 E. 14th Avenue
Columbus, OH 43201
614-294-3296

Chabad House
2350 Secor Road
Toledo, OH 43606
419-535-1930

Oklahoma

Chabad House
6644 S. Victor Avenue
Tulsa, OK 74136
918-493-7006

Oregon

Chabad-Lubavitch
136 S.W. Meade
Portland, OR 97201
503-227-5999

Pennsylvania

Lubavitch Center
7622 Castor Avenue
Philadelphia, PA 19152
215-725-2030

Lubavitch House
4032 Spruce Street
Philadelphia, PA 19104
215-222-3130

Lubavitch Yeshiva
2410 Fifth Avenue
Pittsburgh, PA 15213
412-681-2446

Rhode Island

Chabad-Lubavitch
48 Savoy Street
Providence, RI 02906
401-273-7238

South Carolina

Chabad of Myrtle Beach
6310 Hawthorne Lane
Myrtle Beach, SC 29755
803-449-4843

Lubavitch of Columbia
POB 748
Columbia, SC 29202
803-782-1831

Tennessee

Congregation Sherith Israel
3730 Whitland Avenue
Nashville, TN 37205
615-292-6614

Texas

Chabad House
2101 Nueces Street
Austin, TX 78705
512-472-3900

Chabad-Lubavitch
7008 Forest Lane
Dallas, TX 75230
214-991-5031

Chabad-Lubavitch
6505 Westwind Drive
El Paso, TX 79912
915-833-5711

Lubavitch Center
10900 Fondren Road
Houston, TX 77096
713-777-2000

Chabad House At T.M.C.
1955 University Boulevard
Houston, TX 77030
713-522-2004

Chabad-Lubavitch
14535 Blanco Road
S Antonio, TX 78216
512-493-6503

Virginia

Lubavitch of North Virginia
3924 Persimmon Drive
Fairfax, VA 22031
703-323-0233

Lubavitch of the Peninsula
12646 Nettles Drive
Newport News, VA 23606
804-599-0820

Lubavitch of the Virginias
212 Gaskins Road
Richmond, VA 23233
804-740-2000

Lubavitch of Tidewater
420 Investors Place #102
Virginia Beach, VA 23452
804-490-9699

Vermont

Chabad-Lubavitch
230 College Street
Burlington, VT 05401
802-865-2770

Washington

Chabad House
4541 19th Avenue N.E.
Seattle, WA 98105
206-527-1411

Wisconsin

Chabad House
1722 Regent Street
Madison, WI 53705
608-231-3450

Chabad of North Shore
2233 W. Mequon Road
Mequon, WI 53092
414-242-2235

Chabad House
3109 N. Lake Drive
Milwaukee, WI 53211
414-962-0566

Argentina
(Country Code: 54)

Beit Jabad-Lubavitch
O'Higgins 584
Bahia Blanca 8000
91-49638

Beit Jabad Belgrano
11 De Septiembre 858
Buenos Aires 1426

Lubavitch Argentine Headquarters
Jean Jaures 361
Buenos Aires 1215
1-87-5933

Beit Jabad-Concordia
Uruguay 44
Province De Entre Rios
Concordia 3200
45-21-7898

Beit Jabad-Lanus
Anatole France 1561 1-10
Lanus Este 1824

Beit Jabad-Rosario
Rioja 1449 5A
Rosario 2000
41-64-845

Beit Jabad-Tucuman
Lamadrid 752
Tucuman 4000
81-311-257

Beit Jabad Villa Crespo
Serrano 69
Buenos Aires

Australia

(Country Code: 61)

Beth Rivkah College
14-20 Balaclava Road
Balaclava, 3183 Victoria
3-527-2760

Yeshiva Centre
24-36 Flood Street
Bondi 2026 Sydney NSW
2-387-3822

Jewish House
17 Flood Street
Bondi 2026 Sydney NSW
2-389-0311

Chabad House
883 Centre Road
E. Bentleigh, 3183 Victoria
3-570-6557

Yeshiva Lubavitch
92 Hotham Street
E S Kilda 3183
Melbourne Victoria
3-527-4117

Yeshiva Gedolah
67 Alexandra Street
E S Kilda 3183
Melbourne Victoria
3-527-6733

Ohel Chana Seminary
88 Hotham Street
E S Kilda 3183
Melbourne Victoria
3-527-5461

Austria

(Country Code: 43)

Chabad Center
Grunentorgasse 26
Vienna A-1090
222-311-149

Belgium

(Country Code: 32)

Beit Chabad
Brialmontlei 48
Antwerp 2000
3-187-867

Lubavitch
1a Avenue Reine Marie Henriette
Brussels, 1190
2-345-0522

Brazil

(Country Code: 55)

Yeshiva Machne Israel
R. Coronel Duarte Da Silveira
1246 Petropolis RJ 25600
23-242-4952

Beit Chabad
Rua Serzedelo Correa, 276
Belem, PA 66010
91-225-1994

Beit Chabad
Rua Timbiras, 260/101
Belo Horizonte, MG 30140
31-275-2010

Beit Chabad
Rua Vicente Machado, 1222
Curitiba, PR 80420
41-224-5738

Beit Chabad
Rua Sta Cecilia, 1918
Porto Alegre, RS 90410
512-232-4110

Beit Chabad
Rua Dhalia, 95
Recife, PE 1020
81-325-1475

Rua Pompeu Loriero 40
Rio de Janero 22061
21-236-0249

Tzeirei Aqudas Chabad
P Joao Manuel 758/11
S Paulo 01411
11-282-7868

Escola Lubavitch
Rua Corrca Dos Santos 241
S Paulo SP 01123
11-220-3251

Centro Tiferet
Rua Alagoas 726
S Paulo SP 01239

Beit Chabad Brazil
Rua Chabad 54/60
S Paulo, SP 01417
11-282-8711

Beit Lubavitch
Rua Bom Pastor 514 # 302
Tijuca, Rio De Janeiro
21-286-3782

Canada

Lubavitch of Fraser Valley
2543 Montroso Avenue
Abbotsford, BC V25 3T4
604-266-1313

Chabad of Cote S Luc
5534 Earl Road
Cote St. Luc, Que.
514-489-6022

Hebrew Day School
Cote St. Luc, Que.
514-486-5423

Chabad High
7500 Mackle Road
Cote St. Luc, Que. H4W 1A6

Cong Beth Joseph
44 Edinburgh Drive
Downsview, Ont. M3H 4B1
416-633-0380

Atlantic Jewish County
1515 S. Park Street #304
Halifax, NS B3J 2L2
902 422 7491

Lubavich of Hamilton
87 Westwood Avenue
Hamilton, Ont. L8S-2B1
416-529-7458

Chabad of Chomedy
848 Connaught Circle
Laval, Que. H7W 1N9
514-687-2709

Chabad
1059 Williams Street
London, Ont. N5Y-2T2
519-439-4828

Free Hebrew For Juniors
4649 Van Horne #19-20
Montreal, Que. H3W 1H8
514-735-2255

Chabad Russian Center
6260 Victoria Avenue
Montreal, Que.
514-842-6616

Chabad House
4329 Peel Street
Montreal, Que. H3A-1W7
514-842-6616

Beth Rivka Academy
5001 Vezina Avenue
Montreal, Que. H3W 1C2
514-731-3681

Chabad Centre
4691 Van Horne
Montreal, Que. H3W 1H8
514-738-4654

Rabbinical College
6405 Westbury Avenue
Montreal Que. H3W 2X5
514-735-2201

Chabad House
64 Templeton Avenue
Ottawa, Ont. K1N 6X3
613-820-9484

Anash
31 Albert Street
S. Agathe, Que.
819-326-4320

Lubavitch of Surrey
King George Highway
Surrey, BC

Chabad of Markham
135 Holm Crescent
Thornhill, Ont. L37 5J4
416-731-7000

Chabad House
770 Chabad Gate
Thornhill, Ont L4J-3V9
416-713-7000

Chabad of Kitsilano
3025 W. 5th Avenue
Vancouver, BC V6K 1T8
604-266-1313

Chabad House
5750 Oak Street
Vancouver, BC V6M-2V7
604-266-1313

Jewish Russian Center
18 Rockford Road
Willowdale, Ont. M2R 3V9
416-663-9333

Lubavitch Center
2095 Sinclair Street
Winnipeg, Man. R2V-3K2
204-339-8737

Chile

(Country Code: 56)

Jabad Lubavitch
Eliodoro Yanez 2980
Santiago
2-318-711

Colombia

(Country Code: 57)

Lubavitch
Calle 94 #11-47
Bogota
236-3114

England

(Country Code: 44)

Lubavitch Centre
95 Willows Road
Birmingham B12 9QB
21-440-6673

Chabad Lubavitch
8 Gordon Road
Boscome, Bournemouth
Dorset
BH1 4DW

Lubavitch of Edgware
232 Hale Lane
Edgware, Middlesex HA8 8SR
1-958-8417   1-958-1868

Chabad House
15 The Upper Drive
Hove E. Sussex BN3 6GR
273-21-919

Chabad House
75 Cowley Road
Oxford, Essex
1-554-1624

Lubavitch
361 Cranbrook Road
Ilford, Essex 1G2 6HW
1-554-1624

Leeds Lubavitch
168 Shadwell Lane
Leeds, LS17 8AD
532-663-311

Lubavitch Yeshiva
3-5 Kingsley Way
London N2 0EH
1-458-2312

Lubavitch Foundation
107-115 Stamford Hill
London N16 5RP
1-800-0022

Chabad Lubavitch
3/4 Sentinel Square
Brent Street
London NW4
1-202-1477

Machon Levi Yitzchok
Bury Old Road
Manchester M8 6FY
61-795-4000

Oholei Yosef Yitzchok
Upper Park Road
Salford M7 OH1
61-740-3752

Lubavitch House
62 Singleton Road
Salford, M7 0LU
61-740-9514

France

(Country Code: 33)

Beth Lubavitch
5 Ave Leon Jouhaux
Aix-En Provience, 13093
42-59-06-15

Ecole Chne-Or
150 Rue Andre Karman
Aubervilliers, 93300
43-52-78-49

Yeshiva Tomchei
Tmimim Lubavitch
2 Bis, Avenue du Petit Chateau
Brunoy, 91800
60-46-31-46

Beth Lubavitch
10 Rue Lazare Carnot
Grenoble, 38000
76-46-15-14

Beth Chabad
76 Boulevard De Metz
Lille, 59000
20-54-22-74

Beth Lubavitch
3 Passage Cazenove
Lyon, Arenove 69006
78-89-08-32

Beth Lubavitch
112 Boulevard Barry
Marseille, 13013
91-06-00-61

Beth Chabad Lubavitch
41 Rue Du Rabbin E. Bloch
Metz, 57000
8-7-36-80-88

Beth Lubavitch
5 Rue Bayard
Montpellier, 3400
67-64-37-78

Uforatsta-Lubavitch
19 Boulevard Joffre
Nancy, 54000
8-3-37-22-81

Beth Lubavitch
22 Rue Rossini
Nice, 06000
93-88-57-32

Ecole Sinai-Lubavich
37 Rue Pajol
Paris, 75018
1-46-07-54-57

Bureau Lubavich European
8, Rue Meslay
Paris, 75003
1-48-87-87-12

Beth Lubavitch
8, Rue Lamartine
Paris, 75009
1-45-26-87-60

Beth Chabad Lubavitch
8 Place Jean Moulin
Sarcelles, 95200
1-39-90-82-32

Lubavitch
2 Rue De Niederbronn
Strasbourg, 67000
88-36-46-16

Beth Lubavitch
8 Rue Du Pont Monteaudran
Toulouse, 31000
61-62-30-19

Beth Rivkah
43-49 Rue Raymond Poincarre
Yerres, 91330
69-48-46-01

Holland

(Country Code: 31)

Lubavitch
101 Operaweg
Amersfoort
33-726-204

Lubavitch
Vlaschaarde 59
Amstelveen
20-441-402

Lubavitch
Grevelingen Street 20
Amsterdam
20-794-455

Hong Kong

(Country Code: 852)

Chabad-Lubavitch
27 Macdonnell Road #1B
Hong Kong
5-239-770

Israel

(Country Code: 972)

Chabad Lubavitch of Israel
8-226848

Chabad
15 Ben Ami Street / POB 2564
Acre, 24124
4-714441

Chabad House
2 Kikar Hoatzmaut / POB 26
Afula, 18100
65-592339

Chabad House
37 Chen St
Arad, 80700
57-953330

Chabad House
4 Ashdar Street / POB 667
Ariel, 90920
52-921084

Chabad House
Pan-Lon Bldg. 4 Rogozin Street
Ashdod, 77120
55-22556

Chabad House
714 Shapira Street
Ashkelon, 78100
51-55668

Talmud Torah Chabad
26 Rashi Street
B'nei Brak
3-782441

Chabad House
28 Bareket
Bareket, 73185
3-9721004

Chabad House
67 Hoatzmaut Boulevard
Bat Yam / Migdal Nachum, 59130
3-873673

Talmud Torah
Gan Israel
12 Gershon Street
Be'er Sheva
57-73667

Chabad House
89 Hachalutz Street
Be'er Sheva, 84208
57-38185

Chabad House
19/14 Shikun Chisachon
Beit Sha'an, 10900
65-86884

Lubavitch Youth Organization
Central Office
POB 14
Beit Shazar, 72915
3-985588

Chabad
5 Hatichon Street
Ben Dor
4-234044

Chabad House
POB 218
Ben Gurion Airport
3-9710427

Chabad House
Remez Street
Bet Dagan
3-984784

Chabad House
Merkaz Mishchari / POB 626
Carmicl 20101
4-988915

Chabad House
55/2 Hertzel Street
Dimona 86000
57-59805

Chabad House
POB 36
Eilat 88100
59-77839

Chabad House
11 Shprintzaq Street
Gedera
55-96534

Chabad House
Har Nof
Givat Shaul
2-524098

Chabad House
88 Herbert Samuel Street
Hadera
63-31833

Chabad House
70 Hertzel Street
Haifa
4-674932

Chabad Lubavitch Center
1 Frishman Street
Haifa
4-660549

Chabad House
37 Hoatzmaut Street
Herzelia 46130
52-546146

Chabad House
42 Hasharon Road
Hod Hasharon
52-457211

Chabad House
10 Kikar Weizman
Holon 58322
3-882717

Chabad House
5 Uriel Street
Jerusalem
2-827224

Chabad of The Cardo
1 Cardo
Jerusalem
2-272217

Chabad House
25 Hagana Street
Jerusalem / French Hill
2-815190

Chabad House
Merkaz Mischari
Jerusalem / Gilo
2-764016

Chabad House
POB 26268
Jerusalem / Ir Ganim
2-765221

Chabad House
22 Uruguay Street
Jerusalem / Kiryat Hayovel
2-411206

Yeshivah Torat Emet
16 Yirmiyahu Street
Jerusalem / Kiryat Hayovel
2-814755

Bet Chana High School
19 Ezra Street
Jerusalem / Kiryat Hayovel
2-824955

Chabad House
53 Chabad Street
Jerusalem / Old City
2-283125

Chabad House
7 Shirat Hayam
Jerusalem / Ramot 1
2-868598

Chabad-Lubavitch
POB 8
Kfar Chabad
3-985358

Lubavitch Womens Organization
POB 13
Kfar Chabad
3-984833

Lubavitch Youth Organization
Central Office
Kfar Chabad
3-985588

Kohot Publications
POB 3
Kfar Chabad
3-984018

Central Committee
Kfar Chabad
3-984613

Bet Rivkah Seminary
Kfar Chabad B
3-984571

Chabad House
Beit Shazar
Kfar Chabad
3-984389

Chabad House
128 Weizman Street
Kfar Saba 44102
52-26854

POB 63
Kfar Tavor
6-767384

Chabad House
Lev Hasharon
Kfar Yavetz 45830
52-63055

Chabad
Kiryat Arba 90100
2-961032

Chabad
14 Zevulen Street
Kiryat Ata
4-449033

Chabad House
Merkaz Tzabar
Kiryat Bialik
4-708282

Chabad-Lubavitch
POB 25
Kiryat Gat
51-882493

Chabad House
Block 176/19
Kiryat Malachi Nachlat Har Chabad
55-83799

Chabad House
46-48 Moshe Goshen Boulevard
Kiryat Motzkin 26310
4-732914

Chabad
Kiryat Ono
3-984959

Chabad House
13 Bar Ilan Street
Kiryat Shmuel
4-710042

Chabad House
5 Hachoresh Street
Kiryat Tivon 36111
4-936140

Chabad House
7 Weizman Boulevard
Kiryat Yam 29105
4-755792

Yeshiva Tomchei Tmimim
POB 46
Lod
8-226848

Chabad House
1 Hoatzmaut Square
Lod 71100
8-240280

Chabad House
55 Nachalim Street
Maale Adumim 90610
2-352402

Chabad House
Menahemiya 14945
6-751924

Chabad House
Hoatzmaut Street / POB 267
Migdal Haemek 10552
6-547589

Chabad House
28 Hagaaton Blvd.
Nahariya 22402
4-925410

Mobile Mitzvah Center
POB 1035
Nazaret Illit 11710
65-71468

Chabad House
7 Charod Street
Nazeret Ilit
65-72470

Chabad House
4 Rothchild Street
Nes Ziyonna 70400
54-65624

Chabad House
13 Smilansky Street
Netanya 42120
53-33037

Chabad House
POB 162
Netivot 80250
57-942157

Chabad House
Neve Monison
3-984915

Chabad House
1148 Giborei Yisrael Street
Ofakim 80351
57-922851

Chabad House
POB 117
Omer 84965
57-690903

Chabad House
88 Rothchild Street
Petach Tikvah 49106
3-9227134

Chabad School
9 Hatchiya Street
Rechovot 76110
8-491191

Chabad House
6 Hatchiya Street
Rechovot 76110
8-456817

Chabad House
68 Hertzel Street
Rishon L'tzion 75268
3-992424

Machon Alta
Safed
69-24306

Kirvat Chabad
POB 144
Safed
69-731934

Chabad House
28 Chasam Sofer Street
Safcd
69-31414

Chabad House
Shikun Darom
Safed
69-74005

Chabad-Lubavitch
13 Hadassah Street
Tel Aviv 61162
3-231795

Chabad House
Haprachim Street
Tiberias 14103
67-92402

Chabad House
Merkaz Mischari / POB 224
Tirat Hacarmel 30252
4-573770

Chabad House
10/1 Duane Blvd
Yavneh 70600
8-435797

Chabad
Yesod Hamaleh 12105
6-936186

Italy

(Country Code: 39)

Chabad House
Via Daqnini 24
Bologna
51-340-936

Chabad
Via Genova 26
Ladispoli 00055
6-992-6447

Merkos L'inyonei Chinuch
Via Carlo Poerio 35
Milan 20129

Lubavitch
Via G. Uberti 41
Milan 20129
2-220-490

Lubavitch
Via Lorenzo 11 Magnifico 23
Rome
6-424-6962

Mexico

(Country Code: 52)

Fuente De Ceres 7
Tecamachio 53950
Mexico City 5 D.F.
5-890-656

Campeche 255
Mexico City 7
Mexico
5-742224

Morocco

(Country Code: 212)

Ohale Yossef Yitzhak Lubavitch
174 Blvd. Ziraoui
Casablanca
27 91 95

Juennesse Oufaratsta
174 Blvd. Ziraoui
Casablanca
22 21 46

Collel Avrechim
27 Rue Verlet Hanus
Casablanca 01
27 45 10

Panama

(Country Code: 507)

Chabad Lubavitch
Calle 58 #10 Apt. 5 POB 3087
Panama 3
22-33-83

Paraguay

(Country Code: 595)

Asuncion 660-729

Peru

(Country Code: 51)

Lima

Romania

(Country Code: 40)

Chabad-Lubavitch
Bucharest
Romania
400-150-572

Scotland

(Country Code: 44)

Lubavitch Foundation
8 Orchard Drive
Giffnock, Glasgow G46 7NS
41-638-6116

South Africa

(Country Code: 27)

Chabad Of Lyndhurst
147 Morkel Road
Lyndhurst, Johannesburg 2192
11-640-5100

Lubavitch Foundation
57 Oaklands Road
Orchards, Johannesburg 2192
11-640-7561

Chabad Of Sandton
POB 7861
Gallo Manor
Sandton 2052
11-648-1133

Chabad Centre
6 Holmfirth Road
Sea Point, Capetown 8001
21-44-37-40

Chabad House
33 Harley Street
Yeoville, Johannesburg 2198
11-648-1133

Spain

(Country Code: 34)

Beit Jabad
Calle Jordan #9, Apt. 4D
Madrid 21010
1-445-9629